THE OFF SWITCH:

DISCOVERING YOUR WORK-WORK BALANCE

A DayPack Book

The Off Switch:

Discovering Your Work-Work Balance

By
Steven B. Levy

A DayPack Book

2 4 6 8 9 7 5 3

DayPack Books   ●   Seattle, WA

For Anya, Miriam, and Jeremy: Thank you.

Thanks also to some terrific managers and leaders from whom I've learned so much. Among them are Lew Reines, Jim Stanfill, and Kevin Harrang; each provided leadership in very different organizations that nurtured me for three years or more.

Thanks are also due to many folks who worked for me and who taught me to manage and lead far better than I could ever have discovered on my own. I encouraged them to give me direct and honest feedback; after my head stopped spinning, I eventually figured out how to (mostly) stop doing stupid stuff and to do more work that mattered.

And thanks too, in a very different way, to a few awful managers from whom I also learned much, though perhaps not in the way they intended.

Contents

Introduction

We are the always-on society. On the phone, on the computer, on the go.

We do email like Pavlov's dogs; the new-mail bell dings, the screen exerts its magnetic pull, and our mouths start watering (at least mentally). We check our phones in line, while talking to others, even while driving. We spend hours in ineffective meetings, re-deciding what we thought we'd decided in the previous meeting. We scurry through the warrens of the Internet, chasing after an elusive link (or the latest sports score) as if it were a white rabbit with a pocket watch.

We're trying to ride off in all directions at once.

It's neither fun nor efficient. It isn't low-stress, either.

It's also avoidable, or at least controllable.

What we need is an off switch.

Actually, we need a collection of off switches. Just as each room in the house has its own lights with their own off switches, each of these threats to productivity (and sanity) have off switches.

On and Off: Off switches needn't be all-or-nothing. Small changes can make a big difference.

Attention, Focus, and the Tense Present

Carnegie Mellon professor Herbert Simon wrote in 1971 that "a wealth of information creates a poverty of attention." Forty years on, we continue the wealth-building in terms of the information available to us... and we suffer increasing shortfalls of attention.

People multitask poorly at best, as I discuss starting on p. 20. Rather, we bounce from mini-task to mini-task. Sometimes we put a part of what we're doing on automatic pilot... which works well for breathing and other functions of the autonomic nervous system but works poorly for driving as soon as something out of the ordinary occurs. It works equally poorly for business functions where we need our brain fully engaged.

All of these interruptions and partial-attention tasks lead to stress. We work in the tense present, wondering how and when we'll get to the work that matters, rather than living in the present tense, where results just seem to flow (p. 26).

Flipping a Switch

We can do better, accomplishing more with the same amount of effort. We need to find a few off switches, and flip them.

This book is about identifying those off switches.

These are but switches.
William Shakespeare, *Henry VIII*

Is It a Technology Problem?

No.

It's not a technology problem; it's our problem.

Some of the interrupters and stress factors have technology components, of course. email, phones, the Internet are all technology-based.

But blaming the technology is like blaming automobiles for accidents.

I am not anti-technology. I have four computers that I keep up to date with the latest software. I buy a new smartphone every 12 to 18 months to get the latest features and increased capabilities. I use the Internet, social media, voice over IP (VOIP) phones and video, and more. I love what technology can do for us, and I am committed to taking advantage of it. I am also committed to not letting it take advantage of me.

Some of the off switches are themselves technology-based. Whether or not they have a technology component, however, the key factor in each of them is the human component.

On and Off: Give yourself a low-tech day from time to time – no email, no smartphone, no Internet....

That's you. And me. The knowledge workers and professionals in the business world, the folks who used to be called the white-collar workers.

We hold the key.

We can use off switches, if we so choose, to take back control of so many things in the business environment that are currently controlling us. Sometimes that control is subtle, and sometimes it's overt. Often, it's easier to see the way it affects others than it is to recognize our own reactions.

Do you have enough time every day to accomplish everything you wanted to at work? Are you going home at a reasonable hour? Are you meeting your *big* goals, not just keeping (inordinately) busy?

If not, this book is for you.

(And if you already know how to do what this book suggests, that's terrific; maybe the book can help you explain to a co-worker or colleague what you've been doing and talking about.)

Ready to Jump In?

If so, jump to p. 18. Or you can read straight through about off switches and workplace roles, the book's layout, the Shakespeare quotes, and my qualifications.

We are oft to blame in this; 'tis too much proved.
William Shakespeare, *Hamlet*

Roles in the Workplace

Consider three roles in the professional workplace: assistant, professional, and manager/exec.

Each will find value in this book, I trust, even though they exert different levels of control over their workspace.

Administrative Assistant/Secretary

An assistant (to and individual or a group) is largely reactive, responding to requests both immediate ("get Joe on the phone") and long-term ("plan our October retreat").

While this book isn't specifically aimed at assistants – though of course I'd be grateful if they got their boss a copy! – assistants still need to find connected, concentrated time to complete more complex tasks. Since they are reactive more than initiating workers, there are many interruptions they cannot shed. However, they can still make use of many off switches even with limited control of their environment (see, e.g., p. 66 for a guide to restricting email interruptions to those whose bidding you must do immediately).

On and Off: At times, we play each of these roles; they share problems and off switches.

Professional/Individual Knowledge Worker

An individual professional, such as an attorney, a doctor, a scientist, or a computer programmer, delivers value using her knowledge and training directly, without managing a team (though she might manage an assistant).

Individual professionals can take a huge step by recognizing they *do* have considerable power over their environment. They are paid to bring to bear on problems the power of their intellect; their managers (mostly) recognize that fact, although they may require some gentle reminders (see, for example, p. 178).

Group Manager/Executive

Group managers, team leaders, and executives exert the most direct influence over their workplace. They often own budgets and P&Ls (profit-and-loss statements for their teams); productivity and efficiency reflect directly on them and their bottom-line scorecards.

If you're in this group, you can set the tone for seemingly effortless productivity gains. In fact, perhaps you've been promoted to your current position because you're so effective at getting things done. Either way, as a leader, you can use the lessons of this book to help your team, your customers, and your company – and of course your own continued growth and excellence.

All offices are open, and there is full liberty.
William Shakespeare, *Othello*

Why Should You Listen to Me?

I'm not a theorist. I haven't published academic studies about effectiveness, efficiency, or work-work balance.

I'm a technologist and project manager turned business leader. I've spent a good part of my business career finding ways to help people, departments, and processes become both more effective and more efficient.

I've driven tens of millions of dollars of cost out of systems to make them more productive. I've helped departments full of professionals and knowledge workers become significantly more effective. In the end, the productivity of people has mattered far more than the productivity of systems.

I've managed multi-million-dollar projects to success in many areas. I've taken over and turned around projects that were failing, that were described as doomed. I've started up new departments, and I've taken over existing departments, some of them on the brink of failure.

On and Off: Effectiveness (doing the right things) first; then efficiency (doing things right).

I've run my own businesses, and I've run businesses inside one of the world's largest companies. I've taught professionals and knowledge workers how to think like businesspeople. I've also taught them how to go home at night.

I've led departments filled with hard-working, productive, and happy employees who sought opportunities to work for me again. As a business owner, a consultant, and a "go-fix-this" problem-solver, I've worked with clients and customers to understand and improve loyalty, satisfaction, and effectiveness.

Throughout, I've been practical and pragmatic. I've learned to distinguish what works from what only sounds good; I've always stuck with the former.

For every off switch that's made it into the book, I probably discarded two that didn't work or didn't fit the business world. I was the first subject of most of the experiments that led to these off switches. I then shared them with others, watching carefully to learn what worked for different people. I tried to ensure that my teams weren't adopting them simply because their boss was suggesting them.

Herein are tested off switches. They work in the real world of business; they're not lab experiments.

Not every off switch will work for everyone, but I know some will work for you.

I do serve you in this business.
William Shakespeare, *King Lear*

The Layout of a Daypack Book

A daypack is a backpack in which you carry the essential materials to get through your day. You can easily find things when you need them – a water bottle, something to read, a comb, and so on.

A DayPack book is similar.

It contains the essential materials for a particular business topic, work-work balance and off switches in this case. They are arranged so that you can easily find the material you need in the moment it's most useful.

As with any book, you can read it through, from Introduction to Index. However, you can also pinpoint any topic at the point at which it will be most valuable to you – whether or not you've been reading cover to cover.

The Spread

Many readers tend to skim business books, looking for nuggets of value. Here, these nuggets are called out in an easy-to find fashion, each on its own "spread" of two facing pages.

On and Off: As you read or skim, mark the spreads with off switches you want to try out.

Each spread contains information on one topic relating to work-work balance and off switches. You can read most of the spreads independently, though some cross-reference other spreads.

Many spreads have related information on the preceding or following spread; once you've located the spread you need, you can find other relevant information close at hand.

You might start by skimming the section(s) most applicable to the issues you're facing or areas you want to explore.

As you later meet additional issues or seek more ideas, turn to the spreads germane to those situations.

Gender Words: He and She

There's no perfect way to deal with "he" and "she" in English writing. I chose to alternate them as I wrote, using "he" in one spread, "she" in the next.

The order in which I wrote and rewrote the spreads isn't the same as in the finished, printed book; thus the alternation is no longer exact.

Typesetting

Have fonts gotten smaller, or are our eyes getting older? Either way, I have insisted on a readable font and size.

See them spread, and spread they shall be.
William Shakespeare, *Henry VI pt. 3*

Why the Shakespeare?

What does Shakespeare have to do with off switches?

Nothing. And everything.

First, it's become a tradition in my books. (I try not to repeat epigrams between books, by the way.)

Second, while Shakespeare's plays had plots, of course, most theater people will admit that plots weren't necessarily his strong point.

People were.

Shakespeare understood that theater was about people – the way they interacted, the way they thought, the way they planned and plotted, the way they fell in and out of love, even the way they spoke.

That pretty much sums up management: people management, project management, time management.

The plot drives the play, but the value and strength come from the players and their goals.

Or maybe that's post hoc rationalization. Maybe it's just that I like Shakespeare.

On and Off: Books alone aren't sufficient. **See Will's plays. Try out the off switches.**

My "Rules"

All of the epigrams are taken directly from the plays with no omitted words, and with no changes other than spelling out the occasional shortened syllable such as i' (in), th' (the), and so on. I admit to changing the sense of some quotations by starting them "in the middle" or ending them early. Shakespeare didn't write literally about off switches, so I've taken some liberties.

I have also taken a bit of license with the punctuation, usually to emphasize a point. On the other hand, scholars are at odds about what punctuation Shakespeare intended. The published versions of Shakespeare's plays, the Quartos and First Folio, themselves punctuate almost randomly; neither spelling nor punctuation was consistent 400 years ago.

And though Shakespeare didn't write about work-work balance per se, work-work as well as work-life balance is a theme for many of his characters.

Some, such as Richard II, are over-earnest and wedded to their work; some, such as Falstaff, work hard at avoiding hard work; and some, such as Hamlet and Prince Hal, pretend to the latter while working hard when no one (but the audience) is watching.

Hamlet and Hal, among others, are clear about not mistaking busy for effective.

In your imagination hold this stage.
William Shakespeare, *Pericles*

THE LAY OF THE LAND

MISTAKING BUSY FOR EFFECTIVE

The journey of great leadership starts with a clear vision: where are you going?

To be
too **BUSY**
is some DANGER.

Most of the knowledge workers and professionals I've worked with are busy all the time. It feels like a requirement as a corporate manager, department head, or team leader. Busy, however, isn't the same as productive and effective. Productivity and effectiveness require getting the most important, high-leverage work done, and done well. Burning through 100 to-do items doesn't matter nearly as much as nailing ten (or even two or three) highly business-critical matters.

Management expert Peter Drucker put it this way 45 years ago: "Do first things first, and second things not at all."

In the real world, there are invariably a number of "second things" that we *do* need to accomplish. I offer many suggestions on either doing them, as Drucker says, not at all, or on minimizing the volume of ineffective time you spend on them.

You don't get paid to look busy. You're not even paid to *be* busy, whether you appear so or not. You're paid to accomplish business goals, to make a difference to your organization and co-workers and customers.

Those business goals are Drucker's first things. Remove the distractions and attention-stealing second and third and fourth things that deflect you from achieving them, and you'll reach those business goals... working no more hours (and probably fewer, better-feeling hours).

So many "second things" and they come at us so fast. They keep us busy....

Beyond Work-Life Balance

Many writers, doctors, and HR departments have talked in the past decade about improving work-life balance.

I'm all for such improvement: richer lives, lower stress longer careers without burnout, bringing a wider range of input to bear in the workplace. The off switches in this book will help you maintain and improve work-life balance.

However, equilibrium in the office is at risk from a more insidious imbalance.

Work-Work Balance

Work-work balance is the allocation of time to the various tasks that we must perform in the course of our workdays.

Without off switches, most knowledge workers and professionals are overwhelmed by competing demands on their time: urgent emails, meetings, reports, spreadsheets, forms, and the core work that moves the business forward in terms of revenue, customers, and the products and services that attract them both.

On and Off: Discovering your work-work balance at first takes effort but will become second nature.

If you get to the belated end of your workday stressed by the email you haven't gotten to, the reports you haven't read or written, and the customers you haven't called, how are you going to have work-life balance? At this point, you appear to have but three choices:

1. You can work late, as if you're not working long enough hours already. Obviously, this choice pretty much tosses work-life balance out the window. (Working all evening from home is just a variant of this choice that includes a home-cooked meal... maybe.)
2. You can blow off some of the work, such as leaving emails unread or not returning calls. You can omit parts of your job. While this approach might preserve work-life balance for a time, it portends work difficulties and even job loss down the road.
3. You can do a half-baked job on it all just so you can claim you've touched all the bases. (Don't confuse this approach with "Good. Enough," as described on p. 190). This tack, like the preceding one, isn't likely to keep your ship properly moving forward either.

The Fourth Option: Off Switches

There is a fourth choice, however. You can use off switches to maintain work-work balance, which also supports work-life balance. In the equilibrium of work-work balance, you can do an outstanding job and still go home at night.

The balance of our lives had not one scale of reason.
William Shakespeare, *Othello*

The Myth of Multitasking

Neither computers nor people truly multitask, or perform at full speed two cognitive tasks at the same time.

Most computers simulate multitasking by spending a few thousandths of a second, more or less, on one task, switching to another task and spending a few more thousandths of a second, and so on. It happens so rapidly that we perceive the computer as doing multiple things at once.

Context Switching

Each time a computer switches between tasks, it has to perform a series of save-my-place-and-restore-where-I-was-in-the-other-task operations, called context switching. Computer and software manufacturers have spent decades learning to make context switching faster, but it still costs the computer time. By and large, modern computers, even those in cell phones, are so powerful that we neither notice nor begrudge the time lost to context switching. However, while we may not notice, the time still dribbles away.

Context switching in human beings is another matter.

On and Off: We can't be in two places at once... yet too often we try the electronic equivalent.

We humans are not good at it.

We are not fast at it.

We do not remember perfectly where we were when we return to a task.

The Costs of (Human) Context Switching

There are three huge costs to our own context switching:

1. We lose focus and fumble the ball.
2. We waste time in our already too-busy lives.
3. We get stressed and anxious.

But too much context switching is a requirement of modern life, isn't it?

No. It is not a requirement.

It's the way we live, too many of us, too often.

It's the way we live, but we can improve it. That's what this book is about: improving focus, minimizing wasted or lost time, and reducing the attendant stress.

I don't suggest the methods here will yield perfect focus, zero wasted time, and inner bliss.

But even a small improvement can make a big difference in our lives. Small and even good-sized improvements are goals well within your reach.

Their senses I'll restore, and they shall be themselves..
William Shakespeare, *The Tempest*

Partial-Attention "Multitasking"

Teaching a seminar not long ago, I commented that texting while driving was a clear example of the failure of multitasking. A very bright senior attorney said, "But sometimes you have to." (Even her workaholic colleagues looked askance at that!)

No, you don't have to.

Ever.

You know it's a bad idea, right?

It's easy to recognize in this example that a texting driver is dividing her attention, paying attention sometimes to the cars around her and attention at other times to her smartphone. Perhaps the text message does require only part of her attention (though even that's unclear; see, for example, p. 48).

However, when driving requires your attention, you must attend to it *now*, not when you happen to look up from your smartphone.

Partial attention on the road can kill you.

(Or me.)

On and Off: With partial attention, the sum of the parts is less than the whole.

Experienced drivers allow certain aspects of driving to become background tasks. Our brain filters uninteresting events. (What color was the car on your right 30 seconds ago?) Without conscious thought we subtly adjust the wheel to stay in lane or follow a curve in the road. But the moment an "interesting" situation takes shape, such as a car swerving from the adjoining lane, we focus full attention on it.

We focus full attention... as long as our core attention isn't elsewhere.

Studies show that we can divide attention only as long as non-foreground tasks are routine and repetitive – and only when we remain alert to changes in situation. A braking car while driving, another pedestrian while walking: we avoid them easily if we're alert, but we fail when we're looking at a cell phone (or map or book) while the situation changes.

We pay but partial attention.

We do not multitask; we context-switch (p. 20), focusing for a few seconds on one task and then for a few seconds on another. If the second task demands our attention while we're working on the first, we respond ineffectively.

We know it's the wrong way to drive.

It's also an ineffective way to get work done, no matter how much we fool ourselves into thinking otherwise.

They stared, and were distracted; no man's life was to be trusted.
William Shakespeare, *Macbeth*

John Lennon's Bad Math

In *Come Together*, John Lennon sings, "One and one and one is three." That works for abstract math, but it's wrong in personal-productivity math.

Try this experiment: Find a 15-foot-long "line" on the floor, such as the border between two sets of tiles. Time yourself typing a complex sentence on your smartphone while walking along the line; it's a "fail" if you step off the line. Now time yourself typing the same sentence while standing at one end of the line and *then* walking the 15 feet.

Which took longer?

One and one and one is considerably more than three. Add up the time spent on these tasks (italics represents "time on task"):

> *Time on task #1*
> +   Time switching to task #2
> +   *Time on task #2*
> +   **Time switching *back* to task #1**
> +   *Time on task #1 again*

The sum is clearly greater than if you'd finished task #1 and then done task #2. One and one and one, the three italicized task segments, is greater than three.

On and Off: Background music helps some people focus but micro-interrupts others.

It's even worse in reality than in this simple example; see p. 28.

The cost of switchbacks is staggering. My experience helping professionals free themselves from the trap of the tense present shows interruptions cost at least half an hour per day. Researchers Brid O'Conaill and David Frohlich note that 40% of the time, workers don't even resume the interrupted task; the interruption proves fatal (in the short term) to the first task.

Of course, you cannot complete every single task before moving to the next one when some tasks are hours or days long. However, there are three easy and highly valuable steps you can take to address this question.

1. Divide your tasks so that they are no more than about 20 minutes long, as noted on p. 104. (In effect, create subtasks which you'll begin to think of as separate tasks.)
2. Finish one (sub)task before beginning another.
3. Don't allow yourself to be interrupted. You'll see later that interruptions *are* under your control.

Easier said than done? Sure – but still, it's simpler than you think. That's what this book is all about.

In later sections we'll explore specific off switches for working smarter in a busy world.

Gone, overbearing interruption!
William Shakespeare, *King John*

"In the Zone" or "Flow"

Professional athletes identify the feeling of playing "in the zone." Hitters see baseballs the size of softballs, basketball players see rims four feet across, golfers see holes large enough to contain a cantaloupe.

Hungarian researcher Mihály Csíkszentmihályi defined "flow" as completely focused immersion in a task. You are fully engaged, positive in outlook, and energized, often with the outside world shut out of your awareness.

To be in flow is to be an athlete of the workplace, deep in the zone.

To be in flow is to live for a short time truly in the present tense, escaping the tense present.

To be in flow, or in the zone, is to be focused not on yourself or what's happening around you but solely on the work you're accomplishing. It's your high-productivity zone.

Any doubt that interruptions kill flow?

Right. But what if you're rarely or never in flow?

On and Off: The easiest interruptions to stop are the ones where you interrupt yourself.

Flow and Extraordinary Productivity

Virtually every professional I've worked with has periods of flow. Those who appear extraordinarily skilled have more frequent such times, but it's not clear to me if they are more often in flow because of their skills... or if instead their ability to more easily move into flow allows them to outperform others.

I *have* noted that when most professionals I've worked with remove interruptions and trade the tense present for the present tense, they enter flow more often and do more and better work.

Extraordinary productivity correlates with reduced interruptions. You have the ability to be extraordinarily productive in comparison to where you are today.

You cannot force yourself into the zone... but you can remove at least some of the barriers that keep you from reaching it.

Can you be more productive than everyone else? That's not the point; rather, you can become more productive than you are today.

By the way, if you think flow is hard to come by, watch your child playing a video game. Most kids get in the zone surprisingly easily. College students studying for finals can get there.

Then we enter the workplace and train ourselves out of the habit. What was trained, however, can be untrained.

I'll teach you how to flow.
William Shakespeare, *The Tempest*

Switchbacks: Productivity Killer

"Where was I?"

You hate it when you have to ask or muse about that, don't you? You were doing something, you were interrupted or got sidetracked (or sidetracked yourself), and now you struggle to pick up on what you were doing.

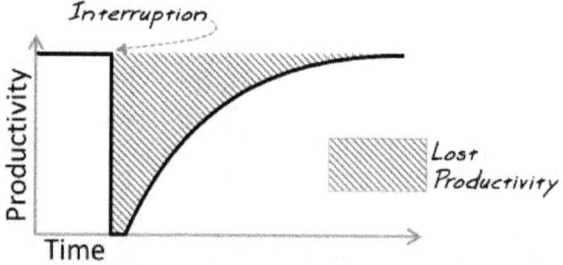

The switchback – returning to an interrupted task – is not only frustrating, it is a productivity killer.

The cost stems not just from the obvious "where was I" search time, though that's bad enough in how it adds to your tense present. However, there is a deeper, hidden cost in the time you spend rebuilding your thought processes and mental structures.

On and Off: email "alerts" are a form of self-inflicted interruption. They're under your control.

What Kind of Work Do You Do?

Let's say you're sweeping the floor, or doing the mental equivalent, work requiring little cerebral continuity. Interruptions to such work have low cost, and might even be welcomed.

However, office work, especially in a professional capacity, requires concentration and continuity of thought. The work you do in a given instant depends on and follows from the work you did in the preceding instants. Lose that sense of continuity, the mental framework you've been constructing, and you often have to drop back two or five or ten steps in your thinking. Switchbacks after interruptions are costly.

How costly?

Research shows it can take as much as 20 to 60 minutes to fully recover from interruptions to highly complex tasks. You don't spend that time at zero productivity, of course, but you are at lower productivity than if you had prevented the interruption or context switch (p. 20). Even the smallest of interruptions, such as noting the blue-tinged alert of an email, can kick off the switchback cycle.

Assume you lose only 1 minute of productivity per switchback. (For most people, that's selling your work short.) If you're interrupted 20 times a day, which is a low number for those who spend much of their day at their desks, that's 20 minutes you can reclaim each day.

There is no time to recover.
William Shakespeare, *The Comedy of Errors*

Stress: The Tiger and the Boat

In a scene in *Apocalypse Now*, Captain Willard and "Chef" (Martin Sheen and Frederic Forrest) are walking through a thick jungle looking for mangoes when they're surprised by a huge tiger. They make it back to the boat safely, and the next shot shows Chef shaking with adrenalin-fueled tension, muttering repeatedly, "Never get out of the boat."

When humans were regularly fleeing tigers, cave bears, and other beasties who thought of us as lunch, we needed to give ongoing partial attention to detecting predators.

There was high tension in this situation. Our limbic system had to be ready to react instantly, the fight-or-flight reaction.

Digestion would slow. Pupils would dilate. Blood vessels would constrict. Nutrients and adrenalin would flow. Tunnel vision would focus on the area of threat. Even hearing would be tuned in only to the threat.

These days, we call those physiological changes "stress."

On and Off: Remember that *real* tigers (business problems) demand full, not partial, attention.

Lions and Tigers and Co-Workers, Oh My

Not all stress is bad, but most of us don't function nearly as well under ongoing levels of tension. What happens when we keep spending partial attention on those parts of the world around us that aren't our focus task? We're willingly slipping out of the boat, maintaining an awareness level well suited for lurking predators.

(I recognize that's how some people would characterize office politics. If you're unfortunately caught up in such an environment, why exacerbate the stress by paying partial attention to those non-predatory aspects of your job that feature an off switch?)

No analogy is perfect. Our body may not really react to incoming email and badly run meetings precisely as if those workplace nasties were big cats contemplating us as food. And even the boat is not a perfect haven, as Chef eventually learns.

Still, why ratchet up the office stress level? What do we gain from such a tense present?

Go ahead, make a list. What's the benefit of constantly jumping out of the boat? We're not *truly* more responsive to customers and co-workers (p. 104). We're less productive (pp. 24, 146). There are other ways to handle micromanaging bosses (pp. 56, 178).

Don't create paper tigers. Worry about the real cats.

Tiger? Take any shape but that.
William Shakespeare, *Macbeth*

What's a "Tool," Anyway?

Traditional dictionaries define "tool" as a device or implement.

A Wider View of Tools

Contemporary society takes perhaps a wider view of tools.

A tool increases efficiency.

A tool can be defined as anything that gives you added leverage (in the broad sense, referring to more than the simple machine by which Archimedes claimed he could move the world).

Consider your kitchen. Obviously a knife is a tool. A set of tongs is a tool. But so is the dishwasher, the stove, the refrigerator; they allow you to be more efficient than you could be with their predecessors.

Even towels, napkins, and cabinets are tools, at least within the wider meanings of tools and leverage.

The definition of workplace tools should be similarly broad.

On and Off: The more broadly you view the tools of the workplace, the more control you'll have.

Tools in the Professional Workplace

There are tools on our computers. Email. Calendar programs, often as part of an email suite. Word processing. Spreadsheets. Internet browsers. Note-taking applications. Project management tools, from task lists to multi-user project schedulers. And most companies and departments have innumerable purpose-built tools such as HR/personnel and accounting systems.

The desktop phone, too, is a tool.

When we leave the desk, we have portable phones that travel with us. We get email on our smartphones. We send and receive text messages. We surf the web, play games, record notes. We sometimes even make phone calls.

Then there are the "non-tool" tools, the leverage engines we often overlook. They too have off switches. We go to meetings. We drop by a colleague's office, or she drops by ours. We have white boards, sticky notes, and flip charts. Our offices have doors – sometimes real ones, other times psychic barriers we can erect or tear down in open-plan workspaces or cube farms. Even an office chair has a type of off switch. (We'll get to it on p. 82.)

We maximize productivity by leveraging our tools effectively. We can learn to use them better.

Sometimes using them better means not using them, for short periods or permanently. We need our off switches.

Having work more plentiful than tools to do it.
William Shakespeare, *Cymbeline*

Summary

Interruptions, divided attention, switchbacks to resume interrupted tasks – they are killing us literally on the roads and figuratively in our offices and workplaces. They are a big part of why we live in such a tense present, a world of frustration, of always busy, of why-don't-I-ever-get-as-much-done-as-I-think-I-should.

In the search for productivity with lower stress, in seeking to work in the present tense rather than the tense present, we need not another time management "system" but to take control of our time.

We need to find the off switch for what defocuses us. The next section looks at the switches we can throw.

On and Off: It's not just devices that have off switches, as you'll see in the next section.

Key Takeaways

- We don't truly multitask; we context-switch.
- Human context switching is inefficient, resulting in dropped assignments, wasted time, and stress.
- Partial attention to multiple foreground tasks is inefficient. (It's sometimes dangerous, too, but this book is about professional-workplace issues.)
- Working "in the zone," in flow, is within reach.
- Switchbacks, the effort spent in returning to an interrupted task, do not add value to the task.
- Interruptions and attendant switchbacks can cost upwards of 30 minutes every day.
- There are three steps to taking control:
    1. Keep tasks to 20 minutes or less.
    2. Finish one task before beginning another.
    3. Don't allow interruptions.

Coming Up...

In coming sections we'll look at specific types of interruptions and other contributors to the tense present: those self-imposed (e.g., email) and those driven by others (e.g., phone calls). More importantly, I'll show you how to take control of the present. You can't eliminate *all* interruptions (you *do* want to hear the fire alarm, don't you?), but you can minimize the way they control your day, your attitude, and your productivity.

By the way, I love email. It's terrific... as long as you use it the way it was originally designed.

> *To be too busy is some danger.*
> **William Shakespeare,** *Hamlet*

EMAIL:

RULED BY OUR TOOLS

Email is everywhere.

It's on your computer. On your phone. On your tablet. You can get it at a hotel or airport kiosk, or even in flight.

Email is everywhere...

...but it doesn't have to be every-when.

Will you
hear
this **LETTER**
with ATTENTION?

Each month, it seems, another revolutionary tool hits the workplace. Like detergent boxes of old, it screams, "New!" "Improved!" "Slices, dices, and cleans up after you!"

The question isn't whether the newest tool can add value. The question isn't even whether the time it takes to learn the tool will outweigh the time it saves you. That's a legitimate consideration, but in few cases does the learning curve overshadow the time you can save – *if* it's the right tool for you.

Rather, the question is this: Can you use this tool effectively to get more done, or to spend less time doing it? Can you use it to add value to your working life? Does it improve business results and strengthen work-work or even work-life balance?

Email as a tool is so ubiquitous, so much a part of the fabric of corporate life, that sometimes we forget it's a tool. As a tool, we can rule it, and overrule it.

It's not the kind of tool you can turn off permanently, removing it from your computer and/or your life. Rather, you turn it off when you're not in need of it, the way you turn off a light when you're not in the room or the room is illuminated by daylight.

In this section, we'll shine some daylight on the nature of email, what it can be at its best, and how to use it to bolster rather than dominate your work-work balance.

Even a few email off switches can repay you with time to get a lot more done. You'll be bucking a trend, perhaps, but that's what leaders do.

The Email Pushmi-Pullyu

The pushmi-pullyu has a head at each end of its body, according to the Dr. Doolittle children's books. Each head tries to lead in its own direction; thus the pushmi-pullyu is hard-pressed to make progress in *any* direction.

Technically, email appears to be a "push" technology: the content is pushed to you, rather than your having to pull it from the Internet. In truth, however, it is beneath the covers a "pull" process, since by default your mail program regularly checks your mail server for new mail and pulls it down to your computer. (It's a bit funkier with an online system such as Gmail or Hotmail, but bear with the metaphor and simplification, please.)

What difference does it make, this push-versus-pull stuff?

Because email is really a "pull," *you can control when it looks for new mail.*

You are not a servant of your email program, as in "But it just keeps showing me new messages." Tell it to stop!

Later, I'll detail multiple ways to do just that (such as pp. 54and 62).

On and Off: Two heads (or tasks) are not better than one when they pull in different directions.

Because the concept of not-always-on-email seems anathema to so many professionals I've worked with, let me suggest another way to view the pushmi-pullyu.

In Character: The Office Professional as Mythical Beast

What happens when you try to "multitask," or divide your attention among more than one primary (focus-intensive or "foreground") task? As I noted above, such an approach ranges from inefficient (pp. 21 and 27) to dangerous (p. 22).

You in effect become a pushmi-pullyu yourself.

One head tries to lead you through one task. The other head tries to guide you through another. You'll likely stagger back and forth between the tasks, caught in time-wasting switchbacks (p. 28).

At best, one head takes control... and drags the other along for the ride in a direction it really didn't wish to go. It's inefficient, hauling half your pushmi-pullyu body (or psyche) along as deadweight, with occasional inner whining that you're not attending to whatever that other head thought was important.

If you're going to be a pushmi-pullyu, at least tell one head to go to sleep for a while! "I'll wake you when it's your turn on task. Now get some rest... and don't interrupt me."

I will be bold with time and your attention.
William Shakespeare, *Henry VII*

The Brilliant Simplicity of Email

A few years ago, I took part in a discussion about future capabilities of email. Among the participants was one of the co-inventors of SMTP, which stands for Simple Mail Transport Protocol. SMTP is the backbone of Internet email. Without SMTP, we'd have no email as we know it.

The group came up with wilder and wilder possibilities. At one point, the SMTP guru said, "Hey, wait a minute. Remember what the 'S' in SMTP stands for!"

He was right in two ways.

First, he was raising a technical issue: email is reliable because the underlying mechanism for delivering it is simple and robust. Overload that mechanism, and it might break down.

He was right in a second way, too, perhaps in a more important way.

Email succeeded brilliantly because it didn't require the participants in a conversation to be present (e.g., on line) at the same time.

On and Off: People's expectations around email differ. You can set/reset those expectations.

The genius of email is that I write when it's convenient and appropriate for me. You read and respond when it's convenient and appropriate for *you*. I can be highly confident, thanks to SMTP, that you will receive my message even if you're home sleeping when I write and send it. Unlike phone calls, we can be on different schedules and still communicate. (Indeed, we did this for centuries via what we now disparage as "snail mail.")

Email works best when we use it as designed. The sender sends on his schedule. Recipients read it on their own timetables. If they choose to reply, they likewise do so when they choose, on their own schedules.

There is no *technological* expectation, as there is with a phone call, that the recipient need be attending to email at the same time as the sender. None. So why do we impose some vague *social* expectation?

When we do so, we not only break the beautiful idea behind email, we break into our own work, our flow, to impose the pressure of the tense present.

Remember what the 'S' stands for. It's simple. The off switch functions beautifully. Even if you, the recipient, have email or your computer turned off, you'll eventually receive the email *when you're ready for it*.

Adding an email "server" such as Exchange or Gmail expands on SMTP technically, but it doesn't change the core idea: simplicity and the resilient off switch.

I with great truth catch mere simplicity.
William Shakespeare, *Troilus and Cressida*

"I Need to Be Responsive"

When I teach email-effectiveness techniques, I invariably hear, "My clients (or customers or managers) expect me to respond immediately to emails."

I'll talk about how to set expectations for co-workers and clients/customers later in this book, in the series of spreads starting on p. 170. I'll also share tips on exceptions ("I can set an off switch for everyone but X") on p. 66.

Here I want to look at responsiveness and perception.

I was explaining the email off switch to a co-worker. He replied, "But Steve, you're always on email!" I know I usually adhere to the main email off switch (p. 54), so together we worked to understand why he had that impression. The table on the facing page illustrates what we figured out.

It turns out that a few times a day we have a flurry of back-and-forth discussion, while the rest of the time his emails sit in my inbox while I'm doing other work. However, that flurry is sufficient for him to *build up the perception* that I'm quite responsive to him on email.

On and Off: Remind clients you might not answer immediately because you're working on *their* behalf.

(I've simplified this example a bit, since we often carry on multiple conversations on different topics. If a single topic does get into serious back-and-forth discussion, one of us will usually pick up the phone, as I suggest on p. 46.)

10:04	He sends me mail
11:15	I begin an email session
11:18	I see his mail and respond to it
11:21	He's always on email, so he replies
11:25	I'm still in my email session and respond
11:28	He sends yet another email
11:29	I answer him, then close email for lunch
11:33	He replies... and I'll see it around 2:30

Responsiveness: Perception Can Be Reality

Co-workers, clients, and customers sometimes want an answer *now*. We've all received "Did you get the email I sent five minutes ago" phone calls, usually from people who mistake urgent for important (p. 190). I've even seen follow-up emails asking, "Did you get my email," which is about as useful as asking, "Are you asleep?"

As noted, I'll cover expectation-setting a few pages south of here. For now, though, recognize that being *at times* highly responsive is part of setting those expectations. This sporadic but regular responsiveness goes a long way toward easing your correspondent's core worry: Will this person (you) really look after my interests?

Answer as I call you.
William Shakespeare, *A Midsummer Night's Dream*

Email "Conversations"

I send you mail at 10:14 A.M.

You reply at 10:16, requiring my response.

I answer at 10:17.

You don't quite agree and offer your thoughts at 10:19.

I don't see it quite that way, so at 10:21....

Silly, right?

Yet we play out this scenario over and over again.

And we do so not just in the workplace but with loved ones, with Internet acquaintances we misbrand friends, with anyone on the other end of our email threads. Outlook and other mail programs even call these interchanges "conversations."

Some conversation.

It's about as effective as the I-should-have-said "conversation" you conduct in your head after an antagonist has left the room.

On and Off: In an email conversation with more than three quick replies? Pick up the phone.

Putting a stop to this practice is absolutely one of the two easiest off switches you can exercise. (See p. 82… where you'll see that I chose the word "exercise" quite intentionally.)

It's not just repeated switchbacks (p. 28) that make such conversations productivity-sappers. It's not the ongoing series of micro-interruptions (p. 48); indeed, often participants in these interchanges await replies with bated breath, meaning that there *are* no micro-interruptions because this slow-motion discussion has become the foreground or focus task.

Rather, the frustration of a slo-mo argument adds significantly to the tense present. With each email you say, "That should clarify it and end the thread." But it doesn't, and deep inside you're probably aware it won't.

The off switch on this conversation? Pick up the phone.

The phone as substitute for email works here only when there are but two or three parties active on the thread. On a discussion list, for example, simply treat it the way you would other email (p. 146).

Sometimes people use email because they're uncomfortable with a more direct exchange. Here's your opportunity to overcome this discomfort: If the other person is active on the "conversation," you know she's ready, right now, to talk about the subject.

See p. 116 for more ideas about this particular issue.

All are banished till their conversations appear more wise.
William Shakespeare, *Henry IV pt. 2*

Micro-Interruptions and Email

Corporate users receive about 75 (non-spam) email messages per day and send about half that much, according to the Radicati Group.

The Radicati survey included a broad spectrum of corporate users; my own somewhat anecdotal research suggests the number is significantly higher for professionals and knowledge workers.

But even the lower number represents almost ten incoming emails per hour.

Ten interruptions per hour.

Is it any surprise, then, that professionals often wonder how to get sufficient real work done (p. 50) amidst the barrage of email? The computer sings out a tone, the cursor morphs briefly into an icon, and (for Outlook at least) the blue ghost of a preview slinks onto the corner of your display, an ectoplasmic apparition that seemingly retreats only when you stare at it long enough to *almost* figure out what the message is about.

On and Off: Of those 10+ emails per working hour, how many are truly important?

Perhaps all this foofaraw made sense when we received only a handful of emails a day. Like mail call at summer camp, it was a special event. Recall Elwood Edwards announcing on behalf of AOL, "You've got mail!" (We'll come back to him on p. 146.) If you checked your email twice a day and received mail only occasionally, it *was* exciting to learn of a new message.

Those days are long gone.

Whenever you are alerted to the presence of a new email, you suffer a micro-interruption. If you pay any conscious attention at all, such as glancing at the blue translucent popup that Outlook offers as a preview, you stagger towards a full-blown interruption.

By considering, even subconsciously, whether to respond to or ignore for now the new mail, you've dealt a blow to your efficiency and productivity.

Partial attention (p. 22) isn't conducive to quality work. Even micro-interruptions represent partial attention. And micro-interruptions distract at least your subconscious mind.

It takes both conscious and subconscious focus to address complex problems. Often the clues that provide insight into such problems stem not from your conscious but from your subconscious mind. Even if you're not "consciously" aware of these micro-interruptions, they're costing you time and productivity.

He that interrupts him shall not live.
William Shakespeare, *Henry VI, pt. 3*

Doing Email vs. Doing Work

Doing email and doing work aren't the same thing.

"But sometimes that's what a manager has to do," I've heard from numerous colleagues and clients: top researchers, managing partners in law firms, corporate executives. "My team has an issue, and I need to jump in and help – *now* – so that they can do their work."

Yes... and no.

I worked for a time for an exec who both humorously and cynically asserted that a manager's job was to forward email. At worst, his comment reflected frustration with people who expected him to solve problems for them rather than connecting directly with the colleague who truly held the answer. At best, it signaled that good managers remove roadblocks to their teams' success.

If most of your incoming emails were urgent, important, *and* appealing for help on problems where your input would be decisive, than email would indeed be a logical place to devote constant attention. (See p. 190 for more.)

On and Off: You wouldn't put "did lots of email" on a weekly personal status report, would you?

I know of no one whose inbox truly has such a profile. (I have worked with a few managers who *believe* it does, but the facts have never supported that belief.)

Managers and leaders should indeed spend time helping their teams with roadblocks (see p. 133), but is that really the core of the job? Rather, you have strategic responsibilities, alliances to build internally and externally, reports to write and analyze, and more.

You cannot do most of that work solely on email.

Worse, email interruptions, both micro and full-scale, limit your productivity on those critical parts of your job. You cannot do the great work you're capable of, the great work CEOs and customers expect of you, with but partial attention. Your work, to say nothing of your customers, your team, and your company, deserves your full attention.

Email isn't the only off switch you can take advantage of, though it may be the most prominent (and, for some of us, the hardest to throw). Use the off switches judiciously on meetings (p. 110), over-brief or overlong tasks (p. 104), tedious reports (p. 128), and even your office itself (p. 82), for example.

Email is seductive; p. 184 shows one well hidden but substantial reason. Resist the confusion and siren song.

I have done my work.
William Shakespeare, *Antony and Cleopatra*

Prove the Email Issue to Yourself

If you're not sure that email interruptions are significant, try an experiment.

Back on p. 49, I talked about micro-interruptions and mentioned Elwood Edwards. Edwards was the voice of AOL, the guy who's "You've got mail!" was immortalized in their software and, later, in one of Tom Hanks' less immortal films.

On the Internet, you can find a sound file of Edwards proclaiming, "You've got mail!" (I found one clip here: http://www.msoutlook.info/files/youvegotmail.wav. While it seems that nothing on the Internet ever truly vanishes, stuff does move; there's no guarantee this link will be valid tomorrow.)

Download it and install it into your mail program as your default new-mail sound, as a short-term experiment.

You can use any speech clip for this experiment; the important part is that it impinge on your conscious mind, which is why I suggest a voice sound clip. (This experiment works better if you have your own office; if you share a workspace, encourage your co-workers to do this experiment with you.)

On and Off: To be doubly annoying, glance at in-coming mail while someone is sitting in your office.

How To (Windows):
◆ In the Control Panel, find Sounds; in Windows 7, choose Hardware and Sound and then select Change System Sounds.
◆ Scroll down in the Program Events box and select New Mail Notification.
◆ Click Browse and navigate to the sound file you want to use. (Hint: Use the Recent Places link near the top of the left-hand panel to find it. Or simply copy the link from the web page and paste it in; Windows will download a copy for you.)
◆ Click OK.

Now each incoming mail will announce itself in a way sure to get your attention… and with all due respect to Mr. Edwards, get your dander up after a few dozen mails.

That's the point.

What you've done is make clear a problem that was likely bubbling just below your conscious awareness level. Just because something is happening in the background doesn't mean it isn't affecting you.

Any sort of new-mail notification is a micro-interruption, whether a sound, the translucent blue ghost, or a flashing cursor. You've just made explicit what had been hidden.

Now go turn your new-mail sounds off (p. 54).

Enforce attention like deep harmony where words are scarce.
William Shakespeare, *Richard II*

The Off Switch for Email

The primary off switch for email consists of two mouse clicks.

Click File. Then click Exit.

File → Exit

Yes, it's simple. And no, it's not easy.

What makes it work is that it's a temporary rather than permanent off switch.

I'm not suggesting you disconnect forever from email. Rather, like a room light, turn it off when you're not using it, when you're doing other work (see, e.g., pp. 26 and 50).

See p. 88 for a discussion of email on smartphones.

The Email Task: Blocks of Time

Email is a task.

Like attending a meeting, creating a report, or analyzing a document, the email task is work with a purpose. As with most tasks, it has specific inputs, outputs, and progress.

On and Off: Addiction (noun): The inability to stop doing something.

Where email apparently diverges is that it lacks a finite scope. When you're done analyzing a document, you're done. You can get through your inbox, but soon it will fill with new mail. You can feel like Sisyphus, forever rolling the rock up the hill only to have it slip from your grasp as you near the crest.

In a way, doing email feels like digging a hole at the seashore. You can scoop it dry, but go spend some time shaping the ramparts of your sand castle and the hole will be full of seawater again.

Yet most of us don't spend the day at the beach staring at the hole, watching for seepage. We scoop it out, sculpt the battlements, and occasionally return to the hole and re-scoop it.

Email is like that hole. Your inbox and the hole *will* fill again. You can't control that any more than King Canute could control the tides. What you *can* control is how you deal with the slow flooding.

To make the off switch work, to bring sanity back to your day, treat email as a scheduled task that recurs throughout the day, each day. It needn't be the same times every day, or the same amount of time in each instance. Set limits, and when the time limit is up, stop.

In the spreads below, we'll look at turning email into a true task, handling exception cases, and gaining efficiency in performing the email task.

The approaching time will shortly fill the reasonable shore.
William Shakespeare, *The Tempest*

Defining the Email Task

There is no one-size-fits-all rule for how often to do email, or for how long at a stretch.

However, there are some guidelines that may prove useful.

Find Your Controlling Factor

How we define the boundaries of our email task(s) depends on which of these four factors affects us most:

1. **Control of schedule:** If you're not in control of your own schedule, you'll have to fit email tasks into your day as best you can, with a different schedule each day and different lengths of time for each block.
2. **Daily schedule constraints:** If you have daily recurring meetings, obviously you'll have to work your email tasks around them. A more subtle constraint is that many days run in 30-minute blocks (a side effect of calendar software); if that describes your work life, schedule email in a few 30-minutes sessions each day.

On and Off: Explicitly put "work time" blocks in your calendar to control part of your schedule.

3. **Culture:** It's hard in some organizational cultures to wean colleagues off the I-expect-you-to-respond-right-now email rollercoaster. In such cultures, you'll likely do better scheduling more frequent but shorter email blocks.

4. **Independence:** If you largely control your schedule and can influence colleagues to accept your email-sanity program (to say nothing of them emulating you and adopting it), you can set up the schedule that works best for you.

As an author and consultant, I fall into group #4 most of the time. When I'm in my office, I do email on average four times a day: in the morning when I sit down at my desk, before lunch, late afternoon before knocking off, and then often *briefly* in the evening, especially when I'm engaged with colleagues in Asia for whom my evening is their daytime. (I'm on the West Coast; were I on the East Coast, an evening session might be valuable to catch up on items important to late-working West Coast colleagues.) In each session, I'll usually empty my inbox (see p. 61 regarding exceptions). When I'm on the road with a client, I do email in the hotel or airport in the morning and at night.

However, when I led departments in the corporate world, I lived in 30-minute blocks. I blocked out early morning and late afternoon "work time" to maintain space in my schedule for both email and "real work". (My assistant knew she could grab these for meetings if nothing else was available; see p. 61.) I'd then find another slot or two during the day on a catch-as-catch-can basis.

Day by day I'll do this heavy task.
William Shakespeare, *Titus Andronicus*

The Email Task: Boundaries

For a moment, assume the amount of email is a fixed quantity for any given week; you will receive and send the same number of messages, with the same content, no matter how you process your email. (This need not be the case, as you'll see on pp. 68, 70, and 190, for example, but it's a valuable "simplifying assumption" for now.)

Thus if it takes you 90 minutes a day to get through email, you could choose to do three 30-minute sessions, nine 10-minute sessions, a 30-minute session and an hour session, etc. In other words, once we have an idea of the length of a good email-task session, we can figure out how many sessions we need each day.

Obviously, not all days are identical, but let's start with simple examples.

Time Limits

Researchers have suggested that task lengths of about 20 minutes are highly productive (p. 104). Consider number that a useful starting point.

On and Off: When doing email, do it! Turn off other distractions and commit to the email task.

How much email can you get through in 20 minutes? If you get through, say, 50 pieces of mail in 20 minutes (most of which are quickly scanned and require no response), and you get 200 emails a day, then you might start with four 20-minute email tasks... in the ideal world.

It's important to schedule time for email (p. 60). Given that so much professional work is locked into 30-minute blocks, it might make sense in many corporate environments to schedule 30 rather than 20 minute email blocks.

Schedules Aren't Perfect

What are the chances you'll get through the last email in your inbox just as your time block ends? Very small, clearly.

The perfect, though, is the enemy of the good. If you end a session with email remaining that you haven't gotten to, it's no big deal. You'll get to it next session. I know it's easy to say "no big deal," but really, it's no different than an email that arrives 15 seconds after you hit the off switch on this email session. If it's a heavy email day and you can extend your task time, that might occasionally be worthwhile; however, don't slide into the trap of all-email-all-the-time.

And if you're done with email before the block is done? That, indeed, is part of the goal, to reduce the time you spend tethered to your email. Over time, you will indeed be able to shorten the time blocks needed for email tasks (see, e.g., pp. 68 and 70).

Hold your session at this time.
William Shakespeare, *King Lear*

Of Schedules and Exceptions

Scheduling Time for Email

Do you track your workday on a tasks-and-times chart, also known as your calendar? If so, email, a task like any other, should have its own slots.

The Visible Calendar: In the corporate world, everyone could read my calendar. This arrangement made it a lot easier for others to schedule meetings. It also made my schedule and activities visible to my teams, reducing misunderstandings. I'd occasionally mark an item private, such as a doctor's appointment. Calendar transparency had many benefits and never worked against me. It made others more efficient when they worked with me... which made me more efficient too.

However, even if you don't calendar it, set a goal of reserving specific times to work on email. If life intervenes on some days and fills your hoped-for email time with crises and appointments, don't give up, falling back into all-email-all-the-time. Try again this afternoon, or tomorrow.

On and Off: Email should serve *you*, don't become its servant.

Don't necessarily call it "Email Time" on your online calendar, especially if your calendar is visible to others. It's "Work Time," or "Get Stuff Done" time. Email is a major task within the block, but email won't always fill the block. Use the remaining time to return phone calls, create necessary reports, and so on.

Making Exceptions

Be willing to cede an email work slot to a more important cause, such as a meeting that's otherwise hard to schedule.

As you start to develop efficient email habits, you may boost peace of mind by adhering to your schedule. Once these habits are established, however, you'll see it as a task with both deadlines and flexibility.

Likewise, if you hit the end of an email task block and still have urgent (and *important* – see p. 190) email work, don't necessarily cut it off. Perhaps you're writing a crucial memo and don't want to derail your train of thought, or you have customer or client mails to which you want to respond before another three or four hours pass. Don't be a slave to either email or the calendar; focus instead on doing the most important tasks at the right time.

Deadlines and cutoffs do instill focus. "When a man knows he is to be hanged in a fortnight," said Samuel Johnson, "it concentrates the mind wonderfully."

But you will take exceptions.
William Shakespeare, *Henry VI pt. 3*

Start Small

As I began to write this spread, I watched a juvenile eagle learning to soar. It took to the sky slowly, making tight loops rather than graceful spirals, flapping its wings more often than an older bird would. After a few minutes, it returned to the nest without prey. It wasn't a successful hunt... but it *was* a successful learning experience.

Like the eagle, I was awkward the first time I "turned off" email, or rather turned it into a real task. Over time I got better. You too can expect to feel odd and awkward at first. You too will get better. You needn't go cold turkey, switching from email omnipresence to task blocks. Start with small steps.

An Easy First Step

If closing your email program feels like a major shift, then put your email window behind the other windows on your desktop, or minimize it to the Windows taskbar or Macintosh dock.

A Simple Second Step

You don't have to shut down email to take this step in turning "Email breaks into my work" into "I do email with control."

> **On and Off:** Email programs begging for attention are poor substitutes for truly being needed.

Start by turning off the features with which email interrupts you: the audible alert, the envelope icon in the Windows taskbar or bouncing icon in the Macintosh dock, and, most of all, desktop notifications, the translucent "ghost" popups that sidle in, steal your attention, and then leave behind only their aftertaste. (On p. 66 I'll show how to let only specific emails whine for your immediate attention.)

You don't need technology skills to disable these so-called features. (They bring to mind the old software joke: What's the difference between a bug and a feature? A feature's intentional.) To turn them off in Outlook 2007 or 2010, for example, choose Options from the File menu and click on Mail, where there's a section titled "Message arrival"; other mail programs, such as Thunderbird and Gmail, have similar settings.

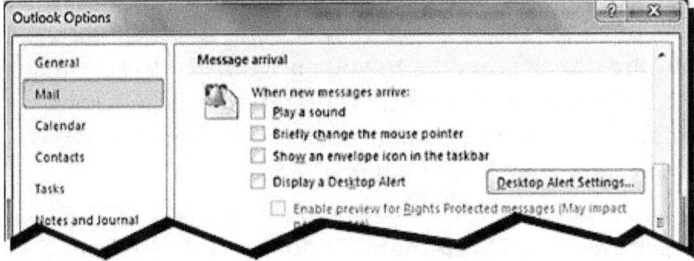

Changing Your Mindset: The On Switch

You can think of email efficacy as an on switch rather than an off switch. Decide when you'll focus – truly focus – on email as a task in itself. Switch it on at those times, and switch it off when you've completed, for now, the email task.

Entreat your grace but in a small request.
William Shakespeare, *Cymbeline*

Being Responsive: Expectations

As I noted on p. 44, some correspondents will have an expectation of immediate response to emails.

While there will inevitably be a few incorrigibles in your sphere, most people will respond favorably to a simple explanation of your email "service level agreement" or "guaranteed response time," especially if they know how to reach you by other means in a true I-need-you-now situation.

Set Expectations Early

It's hard to change established behaviors, though it can be done. Thus it's to your advantage to set expectations early: when you step into a new role, engage a new client or internal customer, etc. All it takes is a very brief explanation:

> **Sample email Statement:** "I do email three times a day, in the morning, at midday, and in midafternoon. I pride myself on responding to email in four business hours. If you need me more urgently, please call my cell phone."

> **On and Off:** Make sure you *are* responsive in email sessions to those who've made requests.

Make sure that you don't contradict your explanation by being on email all the time, saying one thing but doing another.

Adjust Existing Expectations

You can adjust expectations previously set, but it takes a bit more explanation. It's important to let email correspondents know that you're not ignoring them; rather, you're trying to give strategic and mission-critical tasks the full concentration they deserve.

You'll be surprised at how many professionals "get" the fact, at least subconsciously, that email is interruptive and even disruptive. You may even find that they envy your newfound focus.

Discuss your email approach with your manager and your family. Enlist their support. You can often work with a manager to make email efficiency part of your path to the next level; strategic tasks require increased absorption. Then turn it around and let your correspondents know that you're changing your approach as part of your career strategy, with your manager's approval.

If you're a manager of people, projects, or both, make sure your team understands your own work habits, preferences, and expectations, as explained on p. 170.

The hope and expectation of thy time.
William Shakespeare, *Henry IV pt. 1*

When You *Must* Be Reachable

Occasionally you must be reachable by email. Perhaps a client or customer or manager insists on immediate Email responsiveness. Perhaps your family needs your email presence. Or perhaps you're awaiting a specific.

(Aside: What happens if you're in a meeting? Does the customer who wants you to reply in 30 seconds expect you to reply similarly to other customers' emails when you're in a meeting with *her*?)

Instead of casting sidelong glances at your email program, teach it to do the work on your behalf. Use a feature called Rules. Most sophisticated email programs have a powerful Rules component. I'll describe Outlook's here, but others are similar. Note that your email program must be running for Rules to work. Instead of shutting it down, minimize its window when you complete an email task block.

Use Rules to identify certain messages and alert you to them... and only to them. For example, you might alerts on sent by your manager, or where the subject contains certain words. You can create simple rules in Outlook by right-clicking a mail (see the picture).

> **On and Off:** Building a rule isn't hard, but there's a learning curve; practice with simple rules first.

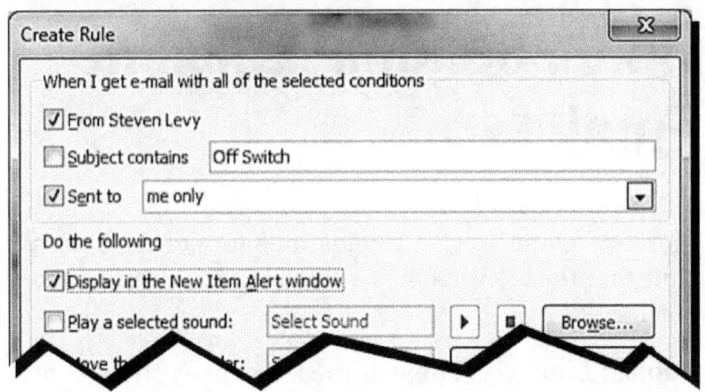

Or you can select Create Rules (under Rules on the Home tab in Outlook 2010), and choose Advanced Options. Set the condition you want to look for. On the next screen select the action you want the program to take, such as "play a sound" or "display a desktop alert" (the translucent blue ghost window).

From is the most important identification clue.

Sent to is useful if you want alerts on messages sent to a distribution list such as "Joe's Direct Reports."

Sent only to me distinguishes mail that no one else has had a chance to reply to.

Where my name is in the To box will ignore mail on which you're only Cc'd, or copied. (Remember the real "Cc," physical carbon-paper copies?)

With specific words in the body (or **...in the subject**) is useful for selecting mail about a particular topic. Note, however, that in Outlook mail will be selected if it includes any of the phrases you list.

They should not laugh if I could reach them.
William Shakespeare, *The Winter's Tale*

Hints: Sending Efficient Email

Here are some simple suggestions for crafting emails that maximize efficiency – yours, the addressee's, or both.

Subject Line: Use subject lines to convey the gist of the message. Doing so allows recipients to quickly determine whether or not they need to open the email now, later, or never. (See also the next suggestion.) Don't be afraid to change subject lines for clarity when forwarding mail, except when there's a potential legal issue at stake. (Dealing with mail when there are questions of attorney-client privilege is beyond the scope of this book.)

If you can convey the entire message in the subject line alone (e.g., "John can't make the meeting"), do so and end the subject line with "EOM" (end of message).

First Ten Words: Summarize the mail in the first ten words or so. Again, this is helpful to recipients who look at the translucent Outlook popup or display the start of the message text in their inbox. Keep the core message short; don't be afraid to relegate supporting material to a "footnote" (i.e., a "details" section below the main message).

On and Off: Help your addressee by being efficient, and over time she'll reciprocate.

Time-Critical Issues: I prefer not to mark messages urgent or high importance, usually indicated by mail programs with a red exclamation point. This is an overused designation that's lost most of its meaning. On the other hand, it's possible to use this indicator for sorting email if it's not abused. My own preference is to put "Time Critical" in the subject line, sometimes with "COB" (close of business) if appropriate. (If you need it sooner than that, drop by the recipient's office, or call.)

Reply-All: Don't reply-all to threads with lots of recipients unless truly necessary. If there's a distribution list on the mail, usually indicated by a boldface *To* or *cc* entry, be extra careful here.

Fonts: Don't use hard-to-read fonts (e.g., script) or lighter colors. If you want an email identity via font and color, stick to readable fonts and very dark colors.

Backgrounds: Don't use a background image or color. Period.

Attachments: Include shorter attachments in the body of the email when possible, to increase the like-lihood the recipient will read them. Warn in the subject line about extra-large attachments, which download poorly over smartphones and slow links.

Expectations: Let the recipient know by when you need a response – which should be at least four hours out, ideally more. And that's four *business* hours, not 9PM for mail sent at 5PM. And if you don't need a reply, sign off with "No reply necessary."

Say in brief the cause.
William Shakespeare, *The Comedy of Errors*

Hints: Reading Email Efficiently

The corollary to using the email off switch is that when you do turn it on, do so at full strength. Don't treat email as a light bulb burning at half-wattage the whole day, not bright enough to fully illuminate the room while you're in it and wasting energy when you're not.

The Off Switch: The first step, of course, is to utilize the primary off switch (p. 54).

The rest of this spread applies to the times when email is switched on.

Newest First: I've found it most efficient to sort my inbox from newest to oldest. That way, if there have been multiple responses to a thread, I can read them together... and also avoid replying to a question that someone else has already answered.

If you're using the email off switch in a corporate environment, there will often be multiple responses before you engage in an email time-block or task... or when you return from vacation. You do not add value (and you waste your own time) when you reply to mail that isn't the latest entry in a conversation (see also p. 190 on "urgency").

On and Off: Trying something new? Give it time (e.g., a few days) before deciding if it's working.

However, you may gain gravitas (the "good" corporate Brownie points) by suggesting a resolution to a fractured or fractious conversation. It's much harder to pull this off if you've contributed to the muddle.

Conversations: You may find value in conversation or thread view, sorted newest first. (In Outlook 2010, it's on the View menu, with options – I select all of them – nearby under Conversation Settings.) Note that some email programs are more effective and space-efficient at this view than others.

Filing vs. Piling: It's possible to divide the world into pilers and filers. Filers sort the mail they save into folders. Pilers use one or two catchall folders – and sometimes use their inbox as the catchall; they use the search function to find what they need.

Neither way is purely better than the other; each has its advantages. (Each also has its acolytes and evangelists who can go on for hours about why their approach is superior.) Don't force yourself to sort if you're a natural piler unless there are legal or corporate requirements that you do so. Likewise, if you're a filer and are under time pressure, don't be afraid to leave email unfiled for a brief time – or, if you must, shunt it to a file-it-later folder.

The Emptied Inbox: Some people are proponents of emptying your inbox at each session. If that works for you, do it. I personally like it, but if this isn't your style, there's more important stuff to get stressed about.

What's the newest?
William Shakespeare, *Macbeth*

"I'm Afraid I'll Miss Something"

Related to the perceived need to be responsive is the fear that you'll miss important information if you're not always on the lookout for it.

First, I'm not suggesting that you reject mail, or ignore it permanently. If you engage in email work sessions three times a day, then you'll be postponing notice of something for, say, four work hours.

Important email

Start by recognizing that you won't miss it per se; it will still be in your inbox in a few hours. Rather, what you'll "miss" is being instantly responsive. As noted throughout this chapter, set clear expectations (pp. 44 and 56, for example), start will small doses (p. 56), and handle exceptions when absolutely necessary (p. 66).

Free Pizza

I grant that there are occasional *real* must-respond-now offers that appear in your inbox. These range from "I've got two seats for the game tonight; first reply gets 'em" to "There's pizza in the break room."

On and Off: Don't mistake "looking busy" for truly *being* both busy and productive.

Keep in mind that a) these offers aren't all that common and b) you won't necessarily respond in time even if you *are* paying attention to those new-mail popups.

Besides, the leftover pizza was probably sitting out in a meeting for an hour, it's now cold, and you already had lunch!

On the Ball

What if you want your manager or co-workers to believe you're on the ball, alert and responsive to whatever they're doing?

There are better ways to demonstrate your importance than "hanging out" on email. Productivity is what matters in the long run. (If your manager is measuring your responsiveness to him rather than results, see pp 169 and 178... and consider if you're in the right job.)

The Latest Jokes, Gossip, and Sports Scores

Okay, I get obsessions. I like to know if the Mariners are winning, or who's leading at the US Open. However, this kind of information is better handled via the Internet (p. 152), where you can control the timing, such as checking the score between task blocks (p. 104). Interoffice jokes and gossip will be just as funny, petty, and frustrating in a few hours as they are now.

What I can help thee to, thou shalt not miss.
William Shakespeare, *All's Well That Ends Well*

Big Trick, Small Trick

Here are two "tricks of the trade" to help build email efficiency and effectiveness.

A Small Trick: Giving the Monkey Back

Are you letting correspondents "put the monkey on your back?" If you get a request from someone and defer it – i.e., can't fulfill it when responding to their message – you've let them give you the monkey. (The concept comes from the work of the late William Oncken.)

Now you've got to carry it around, feed it, and clean up after it. However, sometimes you have just too many monkeys clamoring over space on your back, howling, clawing, screeching. So give a few back temporarily.

1. Send off a quick email asking for more information, e.g., "When do you need this?" They now have the monkey for the next few hours.
2. Tell them when you'll take a first look, e.g., "I'll take a look at this tomorrow afternoon, if that's okay." If it's not okay, they'll let you know (in your next email task block, buying you a few hours); otherwise, you've bought yourself a day or so.
3. Ignore it. (I'm only half-joking; see p. 190.)

On and Off: Pick up *The One Minute Manager Meets the Monkey* (see the Appendix for details).

I don't recommend you do this hidden-deferral trick often. However, if you're truly swamped, it'll buy you time.

A Big Trick: No-Email Thursdays

Organizations might consider announcing No-email days – No-email Thursdays, for example, paralleling Casual Fridays. For this tip to work, the organization must promote the idea both within the organization and to parallel organizations, key contacts, and so on.

Promoting or publicizing No-email Thursdays (or Tuesdays, etc.) includes sharing the reasoning behind the idea... and building support within the organization so that employees truly feel free of email... and don't try to sneak some in. Encourage employees to set up temporary out-of-office messages explaining the concept and resetting the expectations of correspondents.

It doesn't have to be every Thursday. Do it once a month, or for Thursdays until noon.

Perhaps extend the email blackout until 4:30, or until half an hour before the putative "close of business." Employees limited to half an hour for daily email may be surprised at how much they can accomplish in that 30-minute period, especially after the first Thursday when both novelty and trepidation have faded.

Thursday, there is time enough.
William Shakespeare, *Romeo and Juliet*

Summary

Doing email is not the same as doing work.

The email off switch is one of the simplest, yet one of the hardest to truly put into practice. We're wedded to our email, tethered to our computer and through it to our manager, our co-workers, our reports, our colleagues, our customers and clients, even to our friends and family. It tethers us, in fact, to everything but business results.

To achieve work-work balance is to focus more on those business results. But you don't have to work more hours. Rather, control email; don't let it control you. Try out the various email off switches of this chapter. Figure out which ones work for you, and adopt them.

On and Off: Your company may have the right to read personal email sent from your corporate account.

Key Takeaways

- Email is not a substitute for discussion.
- People who do deep-focus email a few times a day can seem as responsive as those living all-email-all-the-time lives. Responsiveness is a perception.
- Set up specific task blocks in which to do email.
- If doing email every three hours is too uncomfortable, start smaller, e.g., once an hour.
- When you're not in your email task, shut it down, or at least minimize the window.
- Turn off the beeps and cursor-changes and popups. They add stress without adding value.
- Tell people how to reach you for urgent-and-important items even when you're not on email.
- All-email-all-the-time on your smartphone is even more problematic, from driving while distracted to working while distracted to trying to type on a small keyboard or touch screen.
- Set boundaries for when and how you do email that start from your need for work-work balance but are consistent with your organization's culture, your manager's style, and your own comfort and stress levels.

Coming Up...

The phone has moved from reliable voice communication to can-you-hear-me-now yelling in public places. Cell phones and desk phones have off switches even as they serve as a backstop to I-need-you-now requests.

Will you hear this letter with attention?
William Shakespeare, *Love's Labor's Lost*

PHONES:

THE CALL OF THE

WILD

"The telephone has too many shortcomings to be seriously considered as a means of communication," according to a Western Union memo from the 1870s.

Some predictions take longer to ripen than others....

'Twere
past all DOUBT
you'd **CALL**.

O pinion is divided on email. Some say it's the scourge of the workplace; some say it has been a workplace revolution; many would hold that both views are valid. But everyone has an opinion about it. Few even think about the humble office telephone.

In some offices, desk phones are disappearing, replaced by cell phones, sometimes augmented by Internet or computer-based (VOIP) calling.

Still, the telephone has some interesting advantages you can leverage in search of increased effectiveness, along with some off switches worth exploring.

As with email, shutting off the phone completely is probably not a viable long-term business option. Indeed, the phone provides a valuable adjunct to email, a way for people to reach you on matters of true urgency (see p. 44).

However, the phone can become a tether too, tying us to interruptive work when concentration and focus, or time with family, would serve us better. It's particularly odd how the cell phone, which gave us the power to roam far from our offices yet remain in touch, has fettered so many people to the immediacy of interruptions rather than freed them from the confines of their cubicle or room.

In this chapter, we'll look at the various off switches for cell phones and office/desk phones, as well as at an efficiency-boosting on switch or two.

If you have questions, leave a message after the beep.

Telephone Off Switches

Telephones have two different off switches. (I'm talking specifically about desk phones; see p. 84 for cell phones.)

Call Waiting

Has there ever been a more frustrating invention than call waiting?

> "I don't know who's on the other line, but by putting you on hold I'm telling you that this unknown person is more important to me than you are."

Granted, with some of today's phones you can see who's calling even when you're already on the phone.

Even a quick check of the caller ID is a micro-interruption, however... and it's one that the person on the other end of the current call can often hear in your voice.

If you lack caller ID, disable the call-waiting feature. Even with caller ID, consider disabling call waiting anyway. You can only be in one place, or on one call, at a time.

On and Off: If you can't disable call waiting, train yourself to ignore its telltale beeps.

The Do Not Disturb (DND) Button

Many office phones have a DND button that sends calls to voice mail without ringing the phone. There are two great times to use it:

1. When you have someone in your office. In fact, you make a significant statement to your visitor that "our time together is important" when you reach over and press the DND button at the start of your conversation.
2. When you absolutely must have uninterrupted focus on a task.

I recommend you limit its use, however, especially if you tell your contacts that you do email only at limited times (p. 54) and that they should call you if they really need a response from you immediately.

So how do you reconcile the second item in the list above, deep focus, with limiting the use of DND when you offer a phone number for immediate response?

You'll find that if you take advantage of available off switches, you'll greatly increase your uninterrupted, high-focus times. If you're not constantly glancing at email, for example, your average level of focus will be higher. You'll find you're regularly completing complex tasks, especially 20-minute high-intensity tasks (p. 104), as part of working normally.

Use your off switches regularly, and you'll have less need to withdraw in order to finish work tasks.

If you will make it an action, call.
William Shakespeare, *Cymbeline*

Cell Phones: Smart Phones?

An increasing number of cell phones today are "smart phones." Games. Internet. Mail. Texting. Phone calls.

People look at them surreptitiously in meetings, during conversations, or even while driving. They check constantly for new email or text messages.

Cell phones are a terrific invention. I live part-time on an island with virtually no coverage, and I worry that my family won't be able to reach me in an emergency. Not everything is an emergency, however. Consider texting while driving. The true message isn't contained in those 140 characters but in the act itself. That message is, "This note is more important than the life of a pedestrian, a fellow driver, or even my own."

As adults with fully developed frontal lobes, we should be able to make this decision clearly and sanely. Still, people are seduced every day by that not-so-smart phone. They regularly make choices that they know are poor, confident that "just this one time" they can get away with it.

On and Off: "Smart" phone is hype. It has a lot of capabilities, but the intelligence must be yours.

Even if we make a poor choice, we recognize that texting while driving is a partial-attention nightmare. Partial attention is *partial* attention. Our work may not be life-and-death, but it is important: to us, to our co-workers, to clients and customers depending on us.

That said, psychologists tell us that warnings about potential consequences are less effective than opportunities to profit by doing the right thing.

So where's the profit?

The Profit in the Off Switch

You can "profit" in three ways by using the off switch on your phone (see p. 86 for ideas on a cell phone off switch beyond simply turning the power off).

1. You can gain efficiency and productivity by eliminating micro-interruptions.
2. Your co-workers will give you more of *their* attention when you stop relegating them to second place behind the call-waiting aspects of a cell phone's new-message buzzing.
3. Your stress level, the tense present, will decrease when you aren't torn between two attention-needed tasks at once (p. 30).

Productivity gains will over time lead to dollars-and-cents profit.

> 'Tis not the first time I have constrained one to call me.
> **William Shakespeare,** *Twelfth Night*

The Cell Phone's Off Switch

The Obvious, Not-That-Useful Off Switch

Clearly you can turn the phone off, or not carry it. (I wonder if knowingly letting the battery run out is a passive-aggressive off switch.)

However, you don't have to go that far, especially when it's also your camera and in-car navigation system.

A More Useful Off Switch

The Ring Tone: The first off switch is the ring tone itself, both your choice of ring tone and your decision whether to have one at all.

When you get a call and your colleagues hear your phone play Wagner's *The Ride of the Valkyries* or Eminem's *Love the Way You Lie*, what does that tell them about you? It carries both an obvious message and a subtle one.

The obvious message, of course, has to do with the song that says "you." Is that really how you want your colleagues to see you?

On and Off: You can hear most phones vibrate even when they're in a purse or in your coat pocket.

The less obvious message is the ringing itself. You come across as less than thoughtful when your cell phone sings out in a meeting. Your reaction to it, also, is telling. Are you embarrassed by it, either by the fact that it's ringing or that it plays *La Marseillaise* in a meeting with your Algerian subdivision? Do you fumble the moment, unsure whether to ignore it, take the call in the face of others, or apologize for the interruption?

By the way, in some cultures it's considered perfectly appropriate to take calls in front of others. That still doesn't mean it's either efficient or good business to interrupt one task with another, spontaneous task.

So, first step: Turn off the ringer. Use Vibrate. (But see p. 110 for notes on cell phones and meetings.)

Selective or Distinctive Ringing: Most modern cell phones will let you associate specific rings with particular numbers. You can use this feature to distinguish calls from your spouse, or your boss.

Unfortunately, few phones let you set up "for the next hour I want only calls from my boss and my spouse to ring." It's an all-or-none situation. Still, there may be occasions where it's okay to have your phone ring but where you don't want to answer it unless it's one of a small set of callers, and you'd rather not look away from what you're doing to see who's calling. Take a minute or two to set up distinctive rings for key people in your life.

Email on Smartphones is covered in the next spread.

You cannot call.
William Shakespeare, *Hamlet*

Email on Your Smartphone

Smartphones – the Blackberry, iPhone, Android phones, Windows Mobile, and others – are astonishing devices. You can check your mail while standing in line, riding in a car (but *not* while driving it, please!), and of course most anywhere you might check it on a computer.

Remember, though, that doing email on a computer isn't always appropriate or efficient.

If doing mail on a computer wouldn't be the best use of your time in that moment, doing so on a phone is likely no better.

Ask yourself, is this the right time to work on mail, either as a discrete task or to capture otherwise wasted time (e.g., standing in line)? If it's not, then it's not the right time to do it on a phone, either.

Buzzing and Beeping Email Alerts

How many times in meetings have you heard the vibrating noise of a phone? Multiple attendees pat their pocket or reach into their purse to see if it's their phone. Usually they'll grin ruefully at each other, but you can do them one better.

On and Off: One of your first tasks on a new phone: learn how to quickly set vibrate and silent modes.

If yours is turned off, you maintain your focus. (Smug grins, however, are frowned on.) Having your phone buzz or beep for incoming email is at least as distracting and counterproductive as having your computer beep when you get email (p. 54).

Three Reasons to Avoid Email on Smartphones

1. It's much less efficient to read and type on small devices or onscreen "tablet" keyboards (iPad, e.g.). If this is the right time to do email and you have access to a computer, use the computer. If you don't have access to the computer but you will shortly, consider whether you could use the current time more productively and defer email for a bit. (Obviously, there will be times where the choice is between email and Angry Birds.)
2. Because it's so hard to type, messages tend to be both terse and less thought through. The former isn't necessarily a bad thing; the latter, though, can be trouble. email can't be unsent.
3. If you're working on formatted email such as a draft report, even the best Smartphones still mess up the formatting from time to time.

One Reason to Embrace Smartphone Email

Productivity. Smartphone email may allow you to make better use of time where you'd otherwise be out of action. Remember, though, that thinking through hard problems is also a good use of "waiting" time.

How smart!
William Shakespeare, *Hamlet*

Living While Distracted

It's just *so* easy.

You think, let me check my mail for a second. Here's a text from a friend telling me about a new movie. And I should text my colleague about looking into that deal a bit further. I wonder if she got back to me in email. Right, now what were you saying?

It should be obvious that I'm shortchanging the person in the room with me.

But I'm also shortchanging myself.

There's a difference between "living for the moment" and flailing. As I've noted earlier (e.g., p. 22), partial attention is both inefficient and stressful.

You deserve better. (And if you won't do it for yourself, then do it for your family and your friends.)

Get over the fear that you'll miss something (p. 72). Except for specific, known-to-be-coming messages (see below), you're deferring, not missing.

You're deferring in the interest of your focus, your efficiency, and your sanity, which are all causes worth contributing to.

On and Off: Treat yourself to a phone-free hour occasionally; then build on that fresh start.

Jack of All Trades, Master of None

Today's always-on devices, in particular those we carry such as smartphones, do lots of things okay, though few of them well. (Unfortunately, making crystal-clear calls doesn't seem to be on the done-well list of most smartphones. Worse, we seem to be adapting to scratchy connections rather than demanding better.)

Good enough is often sufficient (see p. 190), but when it takes no more effort to do better, why not go for it? If you're going to do email in task blocks, do it on your computer, with a keyboard and rich formatting. You'll get more done if you're not tapping on tiny keys or poking at images of buttons. If you're going to play a game or watch a movie, do you really have a better experience squinting at a small screen? (I'm amazed on airplanes when I see someone who has a computer watching a movie on his smartphone.)

Awaiting an Important Message or Call

Remember when fathers-to-be carried pagers awaiting a message that the baby was coming? Often, they'd apologize for the pager, letting colleagues know they were expecting a critical message.

That's still good etiquette: If you're expecting an important message, let people know. If you can, use the distinctive-ring capabilities of your phone (p. 87) to provide an audible differentiator... and then ignore or silence any other interruptions.

A distracted and most wretched being.
William Shakespeare, *Timon of Athens*

Switch Off for Privacy

I'm not one to get excessively paranoid over privacy concerns. Still....

Your cellular provider knows where you are when your phone is on. They know what sites you visit, what movies you watch. That may not be a big deal; it's a requisite part of how cell service works. However, increasingly other parties know where you are, where you've been, and what you've been doing, at least as far as browsing and buying habits go.

Each of us must decide our own level of concern in this regard.

As I write this book in 2011, I'm willing to accept a certain level of what-I'm-doing inadvertent sharing in exchange for convenience. However, I'm not looking forward to the day when text messages with offers start popping up from establishments I'm passing. It's 6 PM, and I'm walking by some restaurants near my home. Dinner offers? Okay... except that I'm just as likely to be heading to the supermarket to pick up food for dinner or the ball field to pick up my son, both of which are in the same area. So are two video rental places, the dry cleaner, and the pet store that carries the overpriced food our dog demands.

On and Off: Even when you're not "on" your cell phone, it transmits its location to your provider.

And that's assuming the various vendors involved can even target me and my overall needs usefully... which, so far, they've proven unable to do.

That's me, however. What about my kids? What will vendors send them? Who will know what about their habits?

As I said, I'm not yet ready to hit the full cell-phone off switch for this reason, but more and more people are unhappy with this situation.

If you're in that latter group, consider protecting your privacy as another reason to turn the phone off – really, full off – part of the time.

The Work-Issued Cell Phone

Do you know the corporate privacy policy on your work-issued cell phone? Does the company have the right to look at phone logs? Read personal emails sent from or received on that phone? Text messages? Can they look at the amount of time you spend playing phone solitaire, or watching movies? Do you want them to see which movies you choose?

Policies differ, both among companies and in different geographies. (European privacy limits in general offer more protection than those in America to employee personal use of corporate resources.)

Understand your corporation's policies.

Fie, privacy, fie!
William Shakespeare, *The Merry Wives of Windsor*

Unplanned Conference Calls

You create an unplanned or spontaneous conference call when you bring another party into an existing phone conversation. You in effect create a spontaneous conference call when, in response to a tangled multi-person email thread, you suggest using the phone to advance the issue and offer to conference in the other folks. These types of calls use the capabilities of your phone or phone system rather than a conference-calling system or software.

At least two situations can benefit if you turn them into spontaneous conference calls: Issues that require input from an additional person (or two), and connecting a person with a problem to someone you think can help solve it.

Unplanned conference calls are an off switch, turning off unproductive email arguments or getting you out of the middle. Of course, you can also ask the participants to call your business conferencing system, but that's asking them to take additional steps, and is fraught with possible mistyped numbers and frustration.

On and Off: Practice a few times with both your office and cell-phone conference-call mechanisms.

Phone-based conference calls are usually easy to set up on office desk phones or computer-based phone systems.

Unplanned Cell-Phone Conference Calls

You can also set up "con calls" on most cell phones. However, as with many cell phone operations, the user interface can be awkward. Thus if you spend significant work time with your cell phone as your only phone, take a few minutes to get familiar with cell-phone conferencing. Learn how to add one or even two more parties to an existing call.

Hint: use the speakerphone function when you're setting up the call, or plug in a headset; it's awkward and frustrating to hold the phone up to your head to speak and listen, lower it to punch in some numbers or menu items, hold it up again, and so on.

Be a Connector: Get Out of the Middle

Organizational strategist Barry Oshry writes about the tendency of managers to "slide into the middle," or become a conduit for information rather than a connector. Bad managers like being in the middle because they feel it makes them essential; the reality is that it makes both them and the process inefficient. If you're talking to someone with a question and know who might have the answer, use a con call to connect them... and then get off the phone, out of the middle, and let them solve the problem while you get work done!

Know the secret of your conference.
William Shakespeare, *Henry VIII*

Useful Phone Tricks

Here are some suggestions on ways to be more efficient using the phone.

Use a Headset

Headsets are the most underused accessory to your phone system. You can keep your hands free for note-taking or other work; their boom microphones minimize background noise when you're in a crowd or a cubicle; and they ease the (admittedly mild) physical stress of holding a phone to your ear or scrunching a handset between your shoulder and your neck.

Use a quality headset with a separate boom microphone (a plastic rod coming from the earpiece), not the cheap earbud-and-microphone-on-the-cable that comes with some cell phones or the Star Trek device that supposedly stays in your ear and picks up your voice through your jawbone. The kind that fit (most) cell phones, portable/wireless phones, and computers cost less than $20. Note that the plug size for most portable phones (2.5 mm) is different from that for cell phones and computers (3.5 mm), but it's easy to find adapters if you don't want to have multiple headsets.

On and Off: Travel with a high-quality headset with a boom microphone for your cell phone.

Note that there are two exceptions. Standard desk phones rarely have headset connectors; you can get special headsets for desk phones, but be prepared for sticker shock. Some cell phones also have one-of-a-kind connectors that require special plugs, though iPhones and Android phones, among others, are leading the charge toward standard (3.5 mm) connectors.

Turn Voicemail Into Texts/EMails

More and more phone systems now offer transcribing features for voicemail, and Google Voice offers a transcribing system for personal and small-office voicemail.

When I get a voicemail, I also get a transcription (sort of) in my email inbox. In addition, I've set up my system to send the transcription to me as a text message, since I am not on email all the time and suggest the phone as the way to reach me more directly.

These systems don't yet transcribe accurately, but usually there's enough information to give you the gist of the call. If in doubt, read aloud what it says; often you can piece together the misunderstood words from the sort-of-sound-alike words the system came up with. These systems usually also include the sound file so that you can listen to the voicemail on your computer, with easy controls to pause it, play hard-to-hear sections over again, etc.

It were a shame to call her back.
William Shakespeare, *Two Gentlemen of Verona*

Summary

Cell phones are near ubiquitous, but that doesn't mean they have to dominate our life. Choose how and when to use your smartphone. Doing a lot of mini-tasks in interruption and short-attention-span mode will not help you get more done, though it may help you feel busy, needed... and stressed.

Nor is that ubiquitous smartphone an effective tool for typing messages. It's fine to love its capabilities when you buy it, but don't get seduced into using those capabilities at all hours just because they're there.

Cell phones and office/desk phones have a variety of off switches you can use to your advantage.

On and Off: We've come a long way since "Mr. Watson, come here. I want to see you."

Key Takeaways

- Call waiting is a feature seemingly designed to insult whomever you're talking with.
- The do-not-disturb button is an off switch best used in very limited circumstances.
- On-my-smartphone-all-the-time is at least as toxic as on-email-all-the-time.
- In business, keep your cellphone on vibrate.
- Put it in silent mode for meetings.
- Turn off email alerts on your phone. Cell phones are supposed to provide freedom, not chain you to the imagined immediacy of others.
- If you *are* expecting an urgent (and important – p. 190) message, let those you're with know.
- Learn more about cell phones and privacy so that you can make an informed decision.
- Learn how to set ad hoc conference calls quickly, to resolve issues or connect problems with solutions.
- Use a good-quality headset with your phone.
- If your voicemail system can transcribe your messages and send them, use the feature.

Coming Up...

It's time to look at productivity in the office. Why is the 20-minute task block so important? How can we make meetings less annoying? What off switches are available from your desk and chair? Work time is time "in the office," whether physically or metaphorically.

'Twere past all doubt you'd call.
William Shakespeare, *The Winter's Tale*

IN THE OFFICE:

THE RIGHT TIME IN THE RIGHT PLACE

The office is where you work... whether surrounded by walls, cubicle barriers, other desks, your car, even your family.

Why,
'tis **OFFICE**
an
of DISCOVERY!

We spend much of our time in "the office." Office as a word means both our individual work base, from a room with a door to a seat next to another road warrior, and the larger workspace shared with co-workers.

The office can also be the virtual or even metaphorical space that houses our desks and computers. It may not even be a constant space from day to day, whether because your office is on the road, your company practices "hoteling" where each day you grab any available desk, or your desk is on wheels and you rearrange the configuration for each project. Especially in these dynamic situations, a key off-switch is learning how to create walls, a door, and a window at the appropriate times.

When we're not in offices, real or virtual, we're often found in conference rooms, real or virtual. As a corporate leader, I would sometimes have "wall to wall" meetings, day after day. I had to learn about meeting off switches the hard way, figuring out how to make meetings more efficient and often shorter, the necessity of creating deep-focus work blocks around the meetings, and even having fewer meetings by learning to delegate properly (p. 184).

This chapter emphasizes three topics each related to the idea of the office: The 20 to 30 minute deep-focus task block, improving meeting efficiency, and making the most of your day-to-day workspace. We'll also take a few related side trips into such topics as OOF (out of the "office") and time-sucking status reports.

It's all just another day at the office.

The 20-Minute Task Target

Studies show we're most effective when we focus on a particular task for 20-30 minutes at a time. Less than that, and we don't reach "flow," that feeling of effortless concentration and efficiency (p. 26). Longer than 30 minutes may be better yet, but not all types of tasks benefit from longer periods, not everyone can deep-focus for an hour or more, and office life sometimes makes it hard to block out more than 30 uninterrupted minutes.

Blocking 20-30 minute uninterrupted periods is one of the most powerful off-switch arrows in your quiver.

Arrange and prioritize both your work and your calendar. The goal is to align your most important tasks with those periods where you can create solid blocks of time.

Perhaps You Can't Do It Alone

In executive ranks, an assistant often manages (and ferociously guards) your calendar. In a small number of jobs you're truly an individual contributor able to work "heads down" for most of the day.

However, most office workers need a bit of help and support, along the lines of the list on the facing page:

> **On and Off:** Don't hide in your workspace; be bold about using task blocks to get more done.

- Enlist your manager.
- Talk with any assistants who schedule meetings within your team; they can become huge allies.
- Block the time on your electronic calendar.
- Do email as a specific task (p. 56) rather than allowing it to be an interrupting intrusion.

Don't get flustered if some of these task blocks get taken by meetings or interruptions. Even CEOs rarely have total control of their schedule, between trying to coordinate with others and dealing with unmovable external events. If you block, say, 15 sessions a week and actually work uninterrupted for 10 of them, you still come out ahead.

It's helpful and reinvigorating to take a small break between task blocks. These breaks can be physical, such as stretching or getting out of your chair (p. 132), or mental, such as checking the score of a sporting event (p. 152). Even something as simple as staring out the window or down the hall for 20 seconds (p. 134) can help you focus on the next task.

Don't Force the Work

If you're stuck on a problem during a task block, don't necessarily force yourself to sit there and stew. Some people feel better when they doggedly pursue an issue; others need to take a break and let their subconscious mind take the reins. But don't use "stuck" as an excuse to check email; rather, find other deep-focus work that needs your attention.

If it make twenty, take them all.
William Shakespeare, *Henry VI pt. 1*

Understanding Meetings

Meetings are both the bane of corporate life and the key to connecting players in the corporate world. Different types of meetings have very different off switches.

Meetings can be divided into two types, individual meetings (usually involving two people, but sometimes three or even four), and group meetings, which involve multiple participants and usually take place in a specific meeting space such as a conference room. Either type of meeting can occur on line or by phone as well as in person.

(There are some additional variants that I won't discuss specifically here, such as spontaneous hallway conversations and presentations to large groups of people.)

Individual Meetings

Individual meetings center either on a two-person conversation (p. 126) or a triad. For the former, sometimes there may be another person or two involved, usually a subordinate, or perhaps someone preparing to step into the shoes of one of the prime participants.

On and Off: Rather than rail against useless meetings, focus them and make them useful.

Triads often have one person "in the middle" (p. 95), where one person connects the person with the problem to someone who might be part of the solution. The third person can also be a mediator (e.g., an HR worker in a personnel discussion) or coach, or someone who's input is needed to make progress on a problem the other two parties are wrestling with.

Group Meetings

Consider group meetings in the context of the matrix on the facing page and the spread on p. 112. Meetings (specifically, each meeting *topic*) have a purpose and a target population.

Purpose: Inform vs. Discuss. Is the purpose to share information or have an open give-and-take? These purposes require different effectiveness strategies and off switches (p. 110).

Involves: Many vs. Few. Does the topic engage most of the attendees, or does it affect only a few of them? In theory, there shouldn't be whole meetings where one or more attendees aren't really engaged; however, it happens, sometimes because of poor time management, sometimes because an early topic unexpectedly turns into fighting a fire, but all too often because of a disorganized, thoughtless, or even arrogant meeting owner.

I defy thee, not willing any longer conference.
William Shakespeare, *Henry VI pt. 3*

Eliminating Meeting Waste

There are seven off-switches for group meetings. (Some also apply to individual meetings.)

Facilitator

Meetings need someone to run them: keep the agenda on schedule (see below), make sure everyone has a chance to speak as appropriate, derail blowhards who can't let go of a topic or "over-share," etc. Often the facilitator is the leader, either the most senior person in the meeting or the person who called it. However, it can be anyone, including an outside consultant. Often the leader's secretary or administrative assistant makes a good facilitator, but the leader must make it clear that this person is empowered to truly facilitate.

Goal(s)

Meetings need a clearly stated purpose. For recurring meetings such as weekly team meetings, the purpose may be implicit; nevertheless, it's a worthwhile exercise to check occasionally if everyone agrees on the goals.

On and Off: Put the meeting goal in the subject line of the meeting notice.

Agenda and Clock

Most meetings need agendas. (For single-topic strategy meetings, the goal is the agenda; p. 110.) The agenda for multi-topic meetings should have timings. The facilitator works the clock explicitly or by ensuring coverage of all topics by meeting's end.

Ground Rules

Ground rules can be implicit in the organization's culture, or explicit, but they should be clear. Who can speak? How is disagreement expressed? (Ideally, attendees disagree with the idea, not the speaker.) Are computers allowed? Cell phones (p. 118)?

Scribe

Designate someone to list decisions, deferrals, and action items – but not to take minutes (see p. 124).

Parking Lot

A parking lot tracks useful topics, issues, and questions that aren't on point for the meeting, would sidetrack the goal, are delaying the agenda, or can best be dealt with separately in an individual meeting, by email, etc.

The Seventh Off Switch

The last off switch deserves its own spread (p. 120).

It remains as the main point of this, our after-meeting.
William Shakespeare, *Coriolanus*

Using Meeting Off Switches

Clear Goals

Either turn off meetings with unclear goals or clarify the goals. If it's your meeting, make sure the goals are clear before you send the meeting notice. (Sometimes email exchanges around trying to set up the meeting will also clarify the goals.) If you're an invitee and don't understand the goals, ask in a non-confrontational way.

Some corporate leaders simply won't attend meetings whose goals are unclear. That's a pretty blunt way to get the message across. I encourage those I coach to be both gentler and more direct, but... whatever works!

Agenda and Clock

If it's not your meeting and you don't know the meeting skills of the leader, you can always ask, "Who will play time cop?" The question serves as a gentle reminder about hewing to an agenda. (Remember, though, that single-topic meetings may not need a timed agenda.)

On and Off: Even casual meetings deserve forethought, even if it happens behind the scenes.

Be a Stand-Up Leader

If it's your meeting, consider doing it as a stand-up meeting if you have such a conference room. In a stand-up meeting, everyone who is able... well, stands up for the duration of the meeting. This strategy may not be loved by all attendees, but it keeps meetings shorter.

If you don't have a stand-up room, you can achieve a similar result by packing people into a small space such as an office.

Ground Rules

Learn to deflect over-sharers, blowhards, hear-me-talkers, and the like (p. 115). See also p. 114 in regard to the opposite "on switch," drawing out those uncomfortable speaking up.

Scribe

Who controls the meeting notes (action items and accomplishments) in retrospect controls the meeting... or at least controls the switches for the next meeting. Even if you're not the scribe, oftentimes it's worth asking to review the notes before they're distributed.

The Biggest Off Switch

Page 120... but by now you probably know what it is.

This is the very description of their meeting.
William Shakespeare, *Cymbeline*

Four Types of Group Meetings

Strategy: Discussion Among Many

Strategy meetings are topic-focused discussions where all attendees (except any separate facilitator or scribe) are expected to contribute. They may be open-ended brainstorming meetings, round-robin state-the-case sessions, or fact-gathering forums such as putting together a budget or estimating project tasks.

These meetings are highly valuable and can be energizing (yes, even budget battles when run well).

Reports: Informing One-to-Many

Often the leader has information to disseminate among the attendees. Sometimes an attendee has a report-out to the other attendees from another group, a committee or project team, etc. While sometimes the information could be shared in email, often there are nuances better conveyed in person (or at least by voice), and a meeting is a better format for questions and answers.

On and Off: Meetings with multiple topics may have *report* or *status* topics; nevertheless, avoid *dilemmas*.

The danger comes from a report-up that is of interest only to a few (see below). If a report becomes too much of a colloquy between two people, step in if it's your meeting. (Even if it's not, gently suggest turning it into a parking-lot item, coming back to it at the end, etc.)

Status: Informing Many-to-One or Many-to-Many

Many people each informing the leader is okay in short bursts in a recurring team meeting. It's valuable for others on the team to know what their colleagues are doing, and the many-to-one really serves as a many-to-many report.

Otherwise, this type of knowledge sharing might be better done in email or separate one-on-one meetings. The determining factor: with most of the other attendees benefit from hearing the report?

Dilemma: Discussion Among a Few

Dilemma meetings are the vampires of meeting-ville, sucking the lifeblood energy out of the room. What do you do if a meeting becomes a two-person discussion (and it's not a "fire," a surprise item that clearly must be dealt with immediately)? If you're a participant in the dilemma, firmly suggest deferring the discussion to a private meeting, or reserving the end of the meeting time for that discussion and giving everyone else some time back. As a meeting organizer, keep dilemmas off the agenda.

I will presently pend down my dilemmas.
William Shakespeare, *All's Well That Ends Well*

Making Group Meetings Work

Beyond minimizing the core meeting wastes described on p. 108, there are two issues that commonly crop up in group meetings: meeting attendees who won't speak up, and those who won't shut up.

Encouraging Others: An On Switch

There are three reasons for not speaking up: corporate culture discourages it (which is beyond the purview of this book), they're afraid the leader will beat on them, or they have cultural or personal reasons for reticence.

As a (meeting) leader, you must encourage them. Praise in public, but correct only in private. Support people even when – especially when – they speak up in a meeting to oppose something you say. Debate ideas, not the other person; meetings aren't cross-examinations or contests. If confrontation is your style, I can't offer reasons you might want to rethink it here (but keep an eye out for my next book on leadership); instead, just go on to the other off switches, which are leadership-style independent.

On and Off: Others learn about you from how you run meetings. See how others see you.

Those who are culturally or personally reticent can over time be coaxed out, but that won't help in tomorrow's meeting. Find ways to connect with them one-on-one, by email, phone, or in person, to elicit ideas. Not only are they likely to have good suggestions, they may be truly excited that you're paying attention, creating a safe environment where they don't feel exposed.

Taking Back Focus: An Off Switch for Others Who Don't Know When to Stop

Some conversations belong outside the meeting:

- Talk to them after the meeting about "selling past the close." That image is often effective.
- Be direct, if that's their style. Tell them they're not giving others the opportunity to talk.
- Coach those who want to fix the habit. Seat them next to you and nudge them when they start going on. (I was coached this way myself; it works.)

Some things you can do in the meeting itself:

- If they're off topic, use the parking lot. "We have a lot to cover, so let's you and I take this up at the end of the meeting, or later in my office."
- Call on others to speak. "Good point, Sue. John, what's your take?"
- Go to the whiteboard and start writing, e.g., summarizing what's been said. Eyes will follow you.

There are whole books about meeting facilitation.

Encourage him not doing it.
William Shakespeare, *The Winter's Tale*

Strategies for Recalcitrants

If you know in advance someone may try to put an off switch on your meeting by taking it over, either directly or by being passive-aggressive, try the following:

Have the Meeting Before the Meeting

Work with him ahead of the meeting to understand and respond to his issues. It's easier to reach agreement when he doesn't feel pressure or a need to posture in a group setting. If he's unalterably opposed, cancel the meeting; don't waste your time and theirs.

Silence Implies Consent

Sometimes you can obviate the meeting (p. 120) by circulating contentious issues in advance. Ask people to reply with any issues or questions, and note that if you don't hear back, you'll move ahead with your plans. Be careful, though; this tack works only with certain people, especially those who feel a need to speak in meetings just so that others will know they're there.

On and Off: Sometimes truly *listening* to people is itself sufficient to resolve the problem.

Milk the Snake

Sometimes objectors need a chance to vent. If you draw off their poison ahead of the meeting, the meeting may go much smoother. Obviously, if the objections are real, you must respond to them (even if the response is "no.")

Honest Graft

Most corporate life is a series of swaps, a quid pro quo of meet-your-needs-and-you-meet-mine. It's "honest graft" when you're helping the other person meet business objectives rather than abetting organizational-politics maneuvering. Often you can find a solution that gives both of you 80% of what you need. Remember that all-or-none, on average, gives you only 50%.

Sometimes these swaps are best worked out ahead of a larger group meeting. At other times, the need for a swap won't be clear until the meeting itself.

Drop the Calls/Walk the Halls

If you need something from someone who'll be in your meeting, consider dropping in on her, especially if she's in your building. Some cultures – especially the high-tech world – are more open to this approach than others. You can often disarm potential issues by visiting the other person on their turf. Especially in today's always-connected world, a personal informal visit can return dividends.

She seems harsh and unwilling awhile, but in the end accepts.
William Shakespeare, *Hamlet*

Cell Phones and Meetings

Which of these are most annoying at a meeting?

1. It's badly run.
2. Attendees lose focus as they check their smartphones (or computers) for mail.
3. Attendees put smartphones on vibrate and place them on the conference room table, where they gyrate noisily when emails stream in.

The good news is that all of these issues are curable. The off switches for badly run meetings (p. 110) take a bit of practice to master. The off switches for the other two items are simple.

If it's your meeting or you're the senior person in the room, ask attendees to shut off their cell phones and close their laptops unless they're using them directly for meeting purposes (e.g., taking notes, gathering budget or sales data, etc.).

If it's not your meeting, ask aloud, "What are the ground rules on laptops and cell phones today?" Just asking the question gets the leader and attendees to think about the issue, which is the first step in increasing everyone's focus level in the meeting.

On and Off: If you have to have your cell phone on vibrate, clip it to your belt or put it in your lap.

In effect, you're sensitizing attendees to the issue; now, when a phone buzzes, its owner will have to think consciously about meeting protocol... and who's looking over at her.

That said, some folks are oblivious. Others believe that their partial attention is sufficient for meeting purposes, or that they are so busy (or so important) that responding to the smartphone's insistent buzz is their highest priority task at the moment.

Indeed, sometimes they're correct in this regard. If so, it's best to be open and overt about it. "I'm expecting a critical message in a few minutes about this multimillion-dollar deal," or, "My wife's expecting any day now."

Attendees Needed for Only Part of the Meeting

Sometimes an attendee is required for only part of the agenda, later in the meeting. If you're the meeting leader, suggest, "Sue, feel free to slide back from the table and catch up on email; I'll get your attention when we hit your part of the agenda." It's also fine to request this arrangement if you're the one not needed until later.

This arrangement makes the practice overt rather than furtive. It also allows everyone to be productive even in multi-topic meetings where some topics are relevant only to certain attendees.

Happy hours? Attend!
William Shakespeare, *The Merchant of Venice*

Off! Alternatives to Meetings

The most obvious off-switch alternative to a group meeting is not having it.

Sometimes it's that easy. Not always, of course, likely not even most of the time, but ask before setting up a meeting, "What will we gain by being in the same room at the same time?" Consider some alternatives to group meetings:

Email: Can we figure out what we need to via email? Email isn't as interactive, but not all meetings truly call for interactivity.

For example, if it's a report or status meeting (see p. 112), where information is being disseminated, can you share the information in email instead?

But... In some cases the team can benefit from being able to ask questions and receive immediate answers.

Multiple Sub-Meetings: If the meeting is largely a series of one-to-one or one-to-two interactive sub-meetings, can you replace each of those sub-meetings with a call or drop-by?

On and Off: The meeting cost is the total time of all participants. Does the value outweigh that cost?

But... keep in mind that teams often struggle or even fail on projects when information isn't shared, when Janet isn't party to a piece of information that Jim hadn't realized she needed or lacked.

Defer: Perhaps the right question is, "Do we need the meeting *now?*" If the need isn't immediate and most of the players likely need to get together in a week or two on another matter, can you combine the current topics into that later meeting? With weekly team meetings, for example, consider if there are weeks where it makes sense to give everyone 30 or 60 (or 90 or 120) minutes back by cancelling this week's meeting.

But... teams do need at least occasional joint "face time" with each other and the leader.

Teleconference or Videoconference: Although online conferencing doesn't change the total collective meeting time, it does simplify logistics and travel time when attendees aren't co-located.

But... Can attendees hear well enough? Do they have access to the right materials? Will they wander into partial-attention mode?

Shorten It: Obviously a shorter meeting is still a meeting, but teams can often benefit by compressing the agenda into a shorter span, such as "being stand-up" (p. 111). Utilize your in-meeting off switches (p. 110).

Assemble presently the people hither.
William Shakespeare, *Coriolanus*

No-Meeting Mondays

I'm not opposed to meetings. Face-to-face exchanges can build teamwork and deliver results unobtainable by any other means. I am opposed instead to inefficient or ineffective meetings.

In addition, too many meetings can leave insufficient focus time – time for thinking about problems and solving them, time for exploring new opportunities, time to build the business.

When I ran departments in the corporate world, I would set a no-meeting day each week. The specific day varied in different departments; I tried to coordinate with groups we partnered with, encouraging their own no-meeting days.

No-Meeting Mondays has a nice ring to it. For companies where work continues over the weekend, reserving Mondays for catch-up is attractive. Other organizations might like the break midweek.

Beyond *Requesting* a No-Meeting Day

I would send my department a recurring meeting invitation for the day in question, 8:00 AM to 6:00 PM. This "meeting" would block off the time on their calendars, showing up as "busy" time when others looked at their scheduling tools.

On and Off: Turn off the reminder when you send a no-meeting-day invitation.

Others outside our department (mostly) wouldn't book them for meetings that day, seeing the time blocked out as "busy."

No-Meeting Days Meet Corporate Reality

The reality of corporate life is that sometimes meetings are scheduled at the convenience of the most senior people in the meeting, with the expectation that others will change their schedules.

Sometimes the logistics of getting multiple people from different groups together becomes impossible without "forcing" the schedule.

And sometimes emergencies occur; if they were both urgent *and* important (p. 190), it was okay to grab a necessary chunk of a no-meeting weekday.

Even with all of these exceptions, the calendars in my departments stayed mostly clear on the no-meeting day. People could get caught up. They could work uninterrupted for long periods of time. They could even schedule and enjoy lunch!

Be Creative

If an entire day is too much, do half-days. If the department as a whole won't adopt it, see if individual managers will... or block off work time in your own calendar.

Beat away the busy meddling fiend.
William Shakespeare, *Henry VI pt. 2*

Taking Notes

Why do we take notes during discussions?

1. To ensure action items are logged and tracked.
2. To make a record of the discussion.
3. Because we got into the habit when we were in school.

Logging Action Items and To-Dos

Tracking to-do items – what, by when, whom – is essential; it's the other reasons that often need the off switch.

By the way, don't confuse logging action items with the far less useful practice of taking meeting minutes (p. 68).

Recording the Discussion

Attorneys and doctors often have a legitimate need to take detailed notes of a conversation. Noting specific facts may be more important than fully joining in the conversation, one time that partial attention (to note-taking and to participating) may actually lead to efficiency.

On and Off: Send a list of decisions and action items after every group meeting.

Most business discussions, though, are as much or more about the relationship than about a scattering of specific facts. Consider putting down the notepad and truly listening, picking it up again for action items or specific instructions.

If you do need to take notes and yet give as much attention as you can to the discussion, consider using a pad and pen rather than a computer. The no-computer off switch creates less of a barrier between participants.

The Old School Tie-Down

Sometimes people take notes because it's become a habit. It's a habit that you may want to switch off in favor of participating with full attention in the conversation.

It's likely that writing it all down will help you recall the information, whether or not you actually review your notes later. However, the cost – partial attention, reduced eye contact, and less true interpersonal connection – often outweighs the small gain in recall.

You don't have to turn note-taking all the way to "off." Rather, consider limiting your note-taking to action items, specific directions received or given (from a client or manager or to a subordinate), and names/contact information.

There's not a note of mine that's worth the noting.
William Shakespeare, *Much Ado About Nothing*

One-on-One/Manager Meetings

I've rarely worked for or consulted to a company whose managers meet often enough with their knowledge-worker or professional employees in a true one-on-one setting.

I can't solve that here. (It's on tap for an upcoming book, though.) However, I do want to offer a few on- and off-switch suggestions for making those meetings more productive when they do occur.

One-on-One On Switches

Agenda: The employee should set the agenda. (See the Vocal Cords off switch on the facing page.) The employee should send it in advance if something on there might surprise the manager or if there's something you want her to think about before the meeting.

Honesty and Trust: Learn to trust; it's the biggest on-switch for strengthening your teams. If trust is granted and then broken, try seriously to repair it rather than sulking; you and the company each have a lot invested in a productive manager/employee relationship.

On and Off: email is great for passing information; face-time builds commitment and finds solutions.

From the employee's perspective, if trust cannot be maintained over time, consider looking for another position. If you're the manager and cannot trust your employee, take responsibility and help him find a position with a manager who might be a better fit. (Outright dishonesty, of course, may require more direct action.)

Clarify: Both parties should clarify what they're hearing. Don't jump to confusions. Do "readbacks," where you summarize in your own words what you think you've heard regarding issues or critical data.

Coaching: One-on-one sessions are great opportunities to coach employees... whether or not the employee recognizes that she's being coached.

The Manager's One-on-One Off Switches

Vocal Cords: Listen first. Seek to understand before you seek to be understood. You have plenty of opportunities to tell your employee what you think, what you want. However, you can't manage without honest and uncensored information from your team, and from those your team partners with.

Clock: Give your team the time they deserve. That doesn't mean an open-ended session, but it takes time to listen effectively. "Be brief, be brilliant, be gone" may be a legitimate style for getting information, but it's less effective for mentoring or coaching an employee.

Businesses: which none without thee can sufficiently manage.
William Shakespeare, *The Winter's Tale*

Off Switch: Status Reports

Few people like writing status reports, and fewer actually read them.

Many status reports are filled with minutiae, such as an attorney's timesheet. The rare reader of this type of report often looks for a loose thread to pull, a minor question on a minor aspect that makes everyone look thorough but adds little real value. Others consist of generalities that differ little from report to report, but the author can "check the box" as completed.

Don't write these reports. Don't encourage them.

However, one status report format is easy to write, easy to read, and usually adds legitimate value.

The 3x3 Status Report

A 3x3 consists of *up to* three brief bullet points under each of the following headings:

- Business value added since the previous report;
- What you expect to accomplish by the next report;
- Present or foreseeable issues, risks, roadblocks, or help needed.

On and Off: Describe the business value you added, not simply the work you did.

The key word is *brief.* If you can't cover it in less than, say, 15 words, you're too deep in the details for the purpose of the report. (Assume the reader has the necessary context and the most recent 3x3 reports.)

People actually read 3x3's. They present the right information simply and directly.

If you or your business partners think status reports will add value, issue 3x3 reports on a regular schedule, usually weekly or fortnightly. (It's time to replace the ambiguous biweekly – is that once every two weeks or twice a week? – with s classic word, "fortnightly," that's fallen by the wayside.)

Don't go longer than two weeks between reports; they'll get too unspecific and harder to compare.

One of the side benefits of the 3x3 report is the ability to compare what you did with what you said you'd do in the previous report.

These should differ occasionally; priorities shift, and new information arises. If they differ regularly, it's a sign that a manager keeps changing what's important or is throwing new work at the team without prioritizing it. These issues stem more often from managers than from those doing the work.

Budgets: If you are reporting on a project with a budget, add a fourth item containing summary fiscal information relative to the budget.

> *All my reports go with the modest truth.*
> **William Shakespeare,** *King Lear*

The Office "Door" Off Switch

All physical workspaces have doors you can close.

Sometimes the doors look like the traditional door shown above. However, even if you don't have a separate one-person office, you have doors you can close.

For example, I've seen teams working in open-plan space, where desk abuts desk, use headphones not just to block out noise but as an implicit sign that they were immersed in high-focus, full-attention work. Sometimes they were actually listening to music, but the headphones signified a door that others respected. (By the way, this doesn't work as well with earbuds. Get real cover-the-ear headphones. Look for those that block or attenuate outside noise.)

I've seen other teams use signs announcing limited availability. For example, some workers seeking to minimize interruptions will post an "Email only" note at the entrance to a cubicle or on a tent card on a desk. (I saw such a note taped to a worker's back. Did he put it there? Did a co-worker attach it as a joke. Maybe I should have emailed him to find out.)

On and Off: If you manage people, use the door sparingly. Be aware of what it says to your team.

Headphones, signs, and other physical indicators, such as a chair blocking a cubicle entrance, are helpful, but body language alone can be effective. If you're obviously deep in concentration, most people will be at least somewhat reluctant to interrupt for non-urgent matters. (Of course, some are oblivious or self-important, but they're not usually stopped by signage or even real closed doors.)

Even crowded coach airplane seats have these doors. Lower your tray table, open your laptop, hope that the person in front doesn't recline his seat, and focus. Don't be afraid to offer a polite "Excuse me, but I have a deadline" to a neighbor after a brief conversation.

Don't Overuse This Off Switch

There's a fine line between focus and withdrawal. If your job requires you to regularly interact with co-workers, don't hide in your office behind closed doors; don't withdraw into yourself at your desk and shut out the world around you.

Rather, use it when you find your workday turning into interruptions that interrupt other interruptions, preventing you from focusing on truly important tasks. Close your door once or twice a day for a 20-30-minute task block (p. 104), or occasionally for a longer period where you need to deliver high-intensity work on an impending deadline.

What's the matter? Will you beat down the door?
William Shakespeare, *Troilus and Cressida*

The Chair in Your Office

The chair in your office has an off switch... even if you don't have an office.

Get up. Move around. It won't count as exercise, but it will make you feel better.

(I recognize that not everyone can get up and move around. As I noted earlier, not every off switch is applicable to all.)

Separation of Tasks

Recall that context switching around interruptions (p. 20) is costly and inefficient.

Similarly, context switching between two full-attention tasks is a process rather than simply flipping a switch.

From time to time, as you round out of one task block and prepare to enter the next, take a brief break from your chair. Stand up. Stretch your arms. Look out the window or down the hall (see the next spread).

The key is that you're doing *something* to mark the transition.

On and Off: The fastest path to office frustration may be an uncomfortable or ill-adjusted chair.

If you've been deeply immersed in a task, your mind will likely linger on items remaining for subsequent work on the task or reflect on your success (or areas for improvement) if you completed the work. Changing your physical position helps signal your mind that it, too, needs realigning.

Even 30 seconds of stretching or standing will pay benefits. Then you're ready to attack the upcoming task block with the intensity and focus it warrants.

Management by Walking Around

If you're a manager of people or projects, take time occasionally between deep-focus task blocks to get out of your chair, away from your desk and office, and practice management by walking around.

MBWA is a real technique, worth exploring if you and your team are co-located. Many managers expect their employees to meet with them in the manager's office, or perhaps in conference rooms. The only time they appear on employee "turf" is when they come down (and it is often down) to deliver a reprimand or vent frustration.

However, if your team is used to your dropping by from time to time, often with no ulterior motive other than to ask how they're doing and to see what roadblocks you can help remove, you'll learn a lot more about the true state of your business. It's said numbers don't lie, but they sure don't tell the whole truth.

I'm very sorry to sit here at present.
William Shakespeare, *Henry VIII*

Sometimes, Stare Out the Window

Sometimes, staring out the window can be an efficiency tool, for two reasons.

As I detail those reasons, I'll talk about how you get around the issue of not having a window to stare out of.

Get Some Eye Relief

Staring at a computer screen all day is tough. Even focusing on it exclusively for an hour or two at a time is difficult.

As with getting up from your chair (see the previous spread), looking for a few seconds at something requiring distance focus is a temporary off switch. It can help you transition between tasks.

Distance focus is what's important here. If you don't have a window, look down the hall. In an open-plan, adjoining-desks office, look across the room. Step out of your cubicle and gaze across the delightful vista of cubes as far as the eye can see. (Or "spy hop" over the top of your cube.)

On and Off: Between tasks, think about what you're seeing; during a task, just relax for a micro-break.

Focusing on something beyond your screen affords both literal and metaphorical value. Not only is it good for your eyes, according to doctors, but it reminds you that the job you're doing exists in a context greater than the confines of your screen.

Perceive From A Different Perspective

If you're stuck on a problem, sometimes obtaining a different perspective can provide a breakthrough. That different perspective need not be related to the problem itself. As you stare at something in the distance, your subconscious will continue gnawing at the problem, often using information and resources you weren't consciously aware you had.

These kinds of quick "look away" mini-breaks aren't interruptions or true context switching, unless you get too caught up in what you're looking at. If you're looking down the hall, for example, and someone waves at you, you'll break your focus; suddenly what had been a background task (gazing) becomes a foreground task (interacting).

Thus while a distance focus is a good between-tasks break, it can be problematic within a task unless you have a place to look that won't truly require your attention. Real windows usually work; if you're in a space with no visual relief, you might put up a travel poster, for example. (Cut the wording off the bottom if you can; words can attract a more conscious focus even if you've seen them a hundred times before.)

Write it all down: such-and-such pictures, there the window.
William Shakespeare, *Cymbeline*

Leaving the Office At Night

How often have you set out to leave work at, say, 4:30, then gotten caught up in one thing after another until yours is the next-to-last car in the parking lot?

It doesn't matter whether you made your 4:30 plan at 8:30 AM and then lost control of your day or decided at 4:20 it was about time to leave and then failed to get away. Either way, you let time manage you and build a tense present.

Without question there are business emergencies that make the best-laid plans, as Robert Burns said, gang aft agley. (And you thought *Shakespeare* was sometimes hard to figure out!) If these "emergencies" are increasingly frequent, you're likely confusing the urgent with the important (p. 190).

The Day-Planning Off Switch

Set a repeating appointment in your calendar for the last 30 or 60 minutes of each day as work time.

These "busy" blocks make it less likely that others will attempt to schedule meetings in that time. Be willing to decline invitations or call into the meeting from your car (hands-free, of course).

On and Off: If your boss wants to see your "commit-ment," send late-night emails instead of hanging around.

Distinguish among true business emergencies (must-do tasks), occasional late meetings with multiple folks who otherwise can't get schedules to align (should do), and urgent-but-not-important sessions (set clear limits). You can't always decline meetings from senior execs, but eliminating at least some of these late meetings yields more control over your day.

Prioritize your tasks so that you can accomplish the most important work early in the day. (It's not about becoming a "morning person," but rather getting to them before today's urgencies pile up.) At day's end, look at what's left; determine if you can defer it to tomorrow or beyond, or perhaps do it at home (but see p. 182).

Most importantly, use your off switches – email, phone, meetings, etc. – to become more productive during the day. Be on the lookout for self-imposed limitations, from looking busy to feeling needed.

The Last-Minute I-Need-You Off Switch

Managers, subordinates, co-workers, and customers all sometimes hit you with urgent late-day requests. Neither invent excuses nor blindly accede to the requests. You can ask, "When do you need this," but instead take the initiative. Offer to have it on their desk at, say, 9:00 AM, giving you the choice of staying late, working from home, or coming in early. That way, instead of saying No or feeling guilty or put-upon, you take some control of the situation.

Came he not home tonight?
William Shakespeare, *Romeo and Juliet*

About That OOF...

Many email programs allow you to set an "OOF" message, for "out of office."

Except that OOF is hardly an acronym for "out of *office*."

Actually, it stands for "out of facility," tracing back to the 1980s and either Unix minicomputers or message slips, depending on whom you believe. (I can buy the idea of some programmer saying, "Let's be inclusive; not everyone actually has an office," and deciding that "facility" would be more comprehensive.)

When You're Out of the Office, Be Out of the Office

Whether or not you set an OOF message on your email, don't be afraid to be truly out of the office, even out of touch (at least somewhat, if you can't throw this off switch all the way). It's easy to carry the office everywhere we go; it's harder to lay it down for a time.

Some emergency responders must be on call all the time. However, as a society we keep broadening the meaning of "emergency."

On and Off: Start slowly. If you can't "let it go" for a day, start with a night, or a few hours. But start.

It makes sense to consider doctors and firefighters emergency responders. It's not unreasonable to stretch the definition to include those whose unavailability would result in work stoppages for many other people – e.g., a relief pilot or a technician for a roomful of computer servers. However, emergency is not equal to "one insomniac manager is annoyed at your unreachability at 3 AM."

Good managers will take the lead in setting appropriate and reasonable expectations for their team. I used to tell my team, "Just because I catch up on email after I put my kids to bed does not mean I expect you to be on email at 11 PM." However, in the end it's up to *you* to set expectations (see p. 64) whether by "managing up" (p. 178) or simply through your actions – and of course it's up to you to support those expectations by being not just responsive but *focused* when you are at work, in the office so to speak.

OOF and "Facility"

Facility doesn't mean only "workplace"; it also means "skill" or "competence." What happens when you're "out of skill," exhausted, running on empty?

If the gas tank's depleted, you need to refuel. Most of us have learned, sometimes the hard way, to keep the needle on our car's gas gauge off of "E." Shouldn't we do the same with our work lives?

Use the available off switches. Get away from the office, truly away, before you run "out of facility."

He drinks you with facility.
William Shakespeare, *Othello*

Summary

Numerous off switches are available to you in the office. Waste less time in inefficient meetings. Be more productive and focused at your desk. Replace unloved status reports.

And most of all, maximize your productivity by setting up uninterrupted and near-uninterruptible 20 to 30 minute task blocks.

Whether your office is surrounded by plasterboard walls, cubicle dividers, other desks, or adjoining seats on an airplane, it's where you do so much of your work. So are the conference rooms, real and virtual, where you exchange ideas and information with co-workers and perhaps customers. Learn to utilize your off switches.

On and Off: Office off switches may be the least obvious and thus the least used.

Key Takeaways

- Align your most critical deep-focus work with scheduled 20-30 minute task blocks.
- Deflect as many interruptions in those task blocks as you can... and don't allow *yourself* to interrupt them.
- Distinguish among meeting types. Avoid "dilemma" meetings (discussion among a few).
- Make sure your meetings have clear goals. If you don't "own" the meeting, be upfront inquiring about the goal(s).
- Understand the meeting ground rules of your organization's culture.
- To maximize meeting efficiency, use the agenda, clock, and the roles of scribe and facilitator.
- Avoid or shorten low-impact meetings. Consider no-meeting workdays.
- Turn off cell phones and email in meetings.
- Instead of meeting minutes, track decisions, deferrals, and action items.
- Use 3x3's for status reporting.
- Go home.
- Your office has a door and a window, even if you need to invent either or both.

Coming Up...

Outside your office is the wide world of the Internet. It's strong gravitational pull necessitates the effective use of off switches.

Why, 'tis an office of discovery!
William Shakespeare, *The Merchant of Venice*

WIDE WORLD:

TO THE INTERNET AND BEYOND

For 15 years or more you've heard all the talk about on-ramps to the information superhighway.

Let's talk about a few off-ramps....

Make
the **NET**
that shall **ENMESH**
them all.

The Internet: source of information, stockpile of unsupported opinion, transformer of the transient into apparent permanence, maze, rabbit hole, timesaver, timewaster.

The Internet off switch doesn't require you to pull the plug. The Internet provides incredibly valuable resources for any business. But it's a tool, and like any tool it works better if you use it effectively.

The off switches of this chapter are designed to help you become more effective in integrating interaction with the Internet into your workday.

Technology changes rapidly. I've tried to avoid writing directly about specific technology in this book, especially evolving technology. Nevertheless, to talk about Internet off switches, I need to talk about the Internet itself. Thus it's possible that some of the specific suggestions here will become outdated in the not too distant future. I have tried for the most part to discuss *approaches* to working more effectively, rather than delving into details of the technological tools that enable such approaches.

I also don't call out social media specifically, beyond a brief note on p. 147. The subject is fascinating, but social media are delivered and accessed through existing mechanisms that already have chapters in this book – email, the phone, the Internet. (Blossoming "addiction" to social media is beyond the scope of this book.)

And remember, the Internet is a great place to learn about books like this one!

The Internet

The Internet is an incredible resource for information (some of it even true), entertainment, socializing, advice, contentiousness, and business connection.

It can, of course, suck up every minute of your day, in which case you probably need a bigger off switch than I can provide. For most people, though, it's a subtle time-stealer. Let me count the ways:

It's Gotta Be There Somewhere: Search engines such as Google can be wonderful tools, but they can also drown you in results that sounded relevant but weren't. We are collectively getting (a little) better at searching, and search engines are getting (somewhat) better at guessing what we're looking for; nevertheless inefficient searching is a productivity killer.

On the other hand, not everything *is* on the Internet. Even the best search cannot find what isn't there, but you can spend a lot of time operating under the belief that "one more search" will turn it up.

Linked to Distraction: Links are one of the coolest things about the Internet. They often lead to fascinating places, charming stories... and delightful wastes of time. Before you know it, you've spent time you didn't have.

On and Off: John Lennon sang, "Thoughts meander like a restless wind" and yet never saw the Internet.

"Just Let Me Check the Score": We can initiate distractions as well as be tempted by them. Who's winning the ballgame? (As a Seattle Mariners fan, I haven't found that a terribly hard question to answer these past years.) What will the weather be tomorrow? What are the lyrics to "Across the Universe"? See the following spread for some ideas.

Every Little Thing: Information overload is a contagious disease. You can get it from the Internet, and you can give it to those asking you for answers. Learn when to stop delving.

Not everything requested of you is a bet-the-company issue. The fourth Internet trap is pursuing every possible angle for the item you're looking into. You can either dive far deeper than the need requires, or you can stall in inaction and indecision because there is so much data – not all valid – on pretty much every side of every issue.

Know when to say when.

Social Media such as Facebook and Twitter are increasingly popular, and increasingly distractive. If you need to see what your friends are doing on Facebook, fine, but don't allow the check-in to interrupt you.

Treat social media alerts the same way you treat email alerts: turn them off on your computer (p. 62) and your cell phone (p. 88). Likewise, check what others are up to the same way you check scores (p. 152): infrequently and without allowing it to distract you even a little from other tasks.

The plain highway of talk.
William Shakespeare, *The Merchant of Venice*

Searching More Effectively

Sometimes finding an answer takes more than just typing a few words into Google. Search engines like Google work surprisingly well at times. They work just well enough that we expect more from them than they can deliver... without our help. Here are a few tips to an off switch for ineffective searching.

Words Vs. Questions

Searching with a lot of words is rarely effective. If you are looking for something with a clear answer, ask a question, such as "how do I turn off sounds in outlook." (Don't worry about capitalization and punctuation.)

On the other hand, if you're looking for information about using Outlook, try simply "outlook" or "outlook tips."

What About Ads and Junk Results?

Search engines often show ads with results, either off to the side, at the top with a slightly different background, or both. Learn to distinguish the ads, or so-called paid search results, from real search results.

On and Off: Even a few simple tips can make searching easier.

Ads are useful if you're looking to buy a product or a service (e.g., someone who can help you with Outlook); otherwise, ignore them.

Junk results are a bigger problem. There are companies that write tons of not-very-useful information around any words they think you might be looking for, so they can sell ads on the result pages. Remember when you encounter one of these "answer farm" sites, and ignore it in the future. On Google, at least, you can also add it to a list of blocked sites.

Search the Right Source

Go directly to sites like Wikipedia for information *about* things, the role of a traditional encyclopedia. Remember, though, that anyone can edit Wikipedia articles. If I'm after critical information, I might start with Wikipedia, but I'll use the references at the bottom of the article to gather more information.

Searching a Site

Often the best way to search a particular site is to use Google or Bing. They search many sites (but not all sites) better than the sites themselves do.

If the search box on the site (e.g., on SomeSite.com) doesn't give you what you need, type the same query into a search engine and append "site:somesite.com" (without the quotes). I'll often start there and not bother with the site's own search box.

Now to the bottom dost thou search.
William Shakespeare, *Titus Andronicus*

Down the Link Rabbit Hole

If you follow enough links, will you eventually reach the end of the Internet?

No, though you may reach the end of your (and your manager's) patience.

Off Switch: Click on Fewer Links

There are normally two reasons for clicking on a link:

1. The link looks interesting.
2. It promises to lead you closer to what you need.

There is some wonderful stuff to be found by pursuing interesting-looking links. Serendipitous browsing can be great entertainment. Rarely, however, will it be useful for work.

In other words, turn off distractions; don't follow irrelevant links, no matter how interesting they seem.

"But I'll never find it again later," you cry.

Perhaps... but first check out a memory chest (p. 156).

On and Off: Right-click links to open them in new browser tabs while retaining your starting page.

Apply this off switch whether the link looks interesting for future business-related needs or for individual enjoyment. Both of these enticements belong in the memory chest.

The off switch may apply even when you're chasing through links in pursuit of your current business task. What you're chasing, according to user-interface researcher Jared Spool, is the scent of information. Do you believe the link will get you closer to your goal? Or are you clicking because you're not sure where to go next, because clicking something is better than staring at the page?

Finding the Right Link on a Badly Designed Site

What do most people want on, say, a restaurant site? The menu, hours of operation, perhaps directions to get there. Yet how many such sites place these items front and center, easy to find?

That's the difference between visual design and information design. (They're not necessarily opposites, though many sites seem to think they are.) Even pure business-oriented sites can have terrible information design, frustrating users. Even for the best sites, there's no guarantee that the obscure bit of information *you* need right now will be prominent.

Don't click random links hoping to get lucky. If the site isn't clear, search it, using either the site's search box or a search engine such as Google or Bing (p. 149).

Now, sir, a new link!
William Shakespeare, *Henry IV pt. 2*

Knowing the Score

The Internet is a near-inexhaustible source of life's fascinations: news, ball scores, celebrity goings-on, Facebook updates, political punditry, weather in Andorra....

There are occasions so momentous that they must interrupt work, even if we each have a different scope for "momentous." The problem begins when sporadic interruptions become an everyday occurrence.

Each person has a different quota of non-work-related time they'll apportion each day. That number is rarely zero; professionals and knowledge workers who spend 10-12 hours or more in the workplace each day usually need to handle various family/personal items during that time. In addition, they often find it refreshing to take a brief break to look at the world beyond work.

The off switch here thus is not elimination of such items, which would probably leave you less happy and thus *less* productive at work.

Rather, the off switch is the control of this time.

Transform the "interesting Internet" from interruption activity to between-task refreshment.

On and Off: Set up feeds for news relevant to your work that you can check daily.

If you're stuck on a problem, you may benefit from giving your subconscious mind a chance to come at the problem from another direction (p. 135).

However, once you let your mind loose on the Internet, you are by default pursuing another task. It's no longer a brief break from which you can seamlessly return; you're in, at best, partial-attention land (p. 22).

Letting the Information Accumulate for You

There are two easy ways to let the web gather information about the events you're interested in, rather than you having to seek them out. (Your computer is much better than you are at the partial-attention thing.)

First, web feeds (called RSS) can bring in all sorts of news items – if you know the sites you're interested in. You can read them easily in your browser and in modern email programs. I subscribe, as it's called, to a variety of business sites, along with neighborhood news and baseball scores.

Second, companies like Google and Yahoo offers "news aggregators," collecting a wide variety of current news (and pseudo-news like celebrity watching). You can personalize them to seek out the types of stories you prefer.

Use RSS and news sites to bring the news to you. (This works well for business-related items, too.)

I shall, in a more continuate time, strike off this score.
William Shakespeare, *Othello*

Know When to Say "Done"

Two traits make it hard, sometimes, to say, "This is done."

First, almost all tasks have a "Done" point that occurs before you simply run out of time to work further on them. Second, "done" and "perfect" aren't synonyms.

We'll look at the latter item on p. 190, tackling the former one here.

The Internet contains more information, rumor, hype, opinion, and error on most topics than we can possibly read through, or even locate. Occasionally there is that one single elusive reference that makes your case, so to speak. It plays out occasionally in the legal world, where a matter can turn on a single obscure precedent from a hundred-year old case. It can also happen in scientific research – but in both science and the law the research takes place more often in specific repositories rather than on the public Internet.

(Medical success may occasionally hinge on Internet findings because anecdotal evidence and one-of-a-kind stories can provide significant diagnostic hints. However, that's the exception, not the norm.)

> **On and Off:** Learn what your manager considers the appropriate level of depth on a particular question.

Once you recognize that you cannot search it all, it become clear you must define a "Done" point somewhere.

Someone is likely asking for the information you're researching, either literally ("how many units did our competitor sell in Arkansas last year?") or as part of a recommendation ("is Arkansas likely to be a profitable market for us?"). That person doesn't want your *research*, but your solution.

It's not how much work you did, but the value of what you learned or accomplished.

Paralysis by Analysis

If Newton were studying the Internet, his third law might read, "For every so-called fact there is an equal and opposite so-called fact." There is so much information in at least partial conflict that it can freeze decision-making.

The inability to get off the dime and decide is called analysis paralysis. We fear to get it wrong.

But as a knowledge worker, you have to decide. Sometimes it's your decision; sometimes you're presenting facts to others.

Either way, you have to make choices about what and how much detail to present. That doesn't mean pushing a bias, but it does mean knowing when to stop looking and act.

There should be "done" amongst us.
William Shakespeare, *Troilus and Cressida*

The Memory Chest

It's said you find something in the last place you look. What if you don't need it at the time you're looking?

It's worthwhile to maintain what I'll call a memory chest.

A memory chest – electronic version – is a place where you can store all sorts of potentially useful or interesting things you run across. Think of it as knowledge management (p. 158) writ small.

There are at least four ways to create one.

Sticky Notes work well for a few items, especially to-do notes you can stick on a whiteboard, monitor, or refrigerator. They're pretty limited otherwise.

Browser Bookmarks also work well for a small set of items. Unlike sticky notes, you can organize them into subsections in a computer-folder structure.

Browser bookmarks or favorites work well for many people, especially those who are pilers rather than filers (p. 70). However, they capture only location, not the content itself, by remembering Internet pages. They also don't help you find something within long pages.

On and Off: Use your memory chest to save short-term, I-want-to-look-at-this-later items as well.

For example, my memory chest holds not just links but notes I've taken, quotes I find interesting, pictures of what's on my computer screen, and more. Bookmarks don't accommodate that extended inventory.

Online Citation Programs such as iCyte are a more flexible version of bookmarks, but ultimately they're still websites rather than general-purpose memory. They're subject to the many of the same limitations, however.

I also worry how long these sites will be around; if the site goes out of business, will my information be accessible?

Note-Taking Programs such as OneNote and Evernote combine the benefits of the other three methods

As I write this, OneNote is included at no extra cost with Microsoft Office, and Evernote has a free version. Both run on multiple devices, meaning that you can take notes and view notes on your smartphone that are tied to your computer.

I find these kinds of programs essential. I use OneNote not just for taking notes on calls and in meetings but as my memory chest. I track quotes, minutes of a board of trustees on which I serve, ideas, client pricing information, screenshots, and much more. (It even backs up automatically to the web and synchs across my various computers.

It unlinked itself and, with intended glides, did slip away.
William Shakespeare, *As You Like It*

Asking for Help

Asking for help is a "weighty" question; you have to weigh the pros and cons, especially when responses can range from curmudgeonly resentment to gratitude (or "brag-itude") for offering a chance to show expertise.

The Cons of Asking for Help

- Others may see you as less than competent, which could affect your career trajectory.
- Others might be offended that you treat their time as less valuable by not working harder to figure it out yourself.
- You usually learn more by figuring it out yourself… as long as you *do* figure it out, and come up with a sound solution.

The Pros of Asking for Help

- You get the answer faster
- You may get a better answer, either because the other person is more knowledgeable or because two heads are better than one for some problems.
- You make contacts that may encourage teamwork, sharing, and perhaps others trusting that you won't disparage them should they come to *you* for help.

On and Off: Find a middle ground. Try to solve it yourself, but don't waste hours on a ten-minute issue.

The last point is the foundation on which knowledge management can be built.

Knowledge Management

Knowledge management systems fall somewhere between the Holy Grail and a shibboleth in many organizations. Don't mistake KM systems, however, for knowledge management itself.

True KM includes not just purpose-built software but searching the Internet, looking through public and private databases (e.g., attorneys researching cases on LexisNexis), combing internal data (intranet, file shares, even your own hard drive and memory chest), and asking someone.

The key to KM is "give to get."

If you hoard your knowledge, why would others share with you? Yet many organizations foster a culture of knowledge hoarding, albeit not always intentionally; those who get ahead are those with "hidden knowledge" of how systems really work, of how to work the system, or where the figurative bodies are buried.

Unless your culture truly frowns on knowledge sharing, knowledge and expertise should be an on switch, not an off switch. Share willingly. Ask when appropriate. (And do so as schedules permit rather than by interruption.)

You shall come to clearer knowledge.
William Shakespeare, *The Winter's Tale*

Summary

The Internet is both timesaver extraordinaire and sneaky timewaster... often apparently at the same time. Like fire, it both warms and burns.

The Internet differs from cell phones and email in that it doesn't grab your attention by beeping, buzzing, ringing, or playing a song that you really didn't want your co-workers to know you liked. Rather, you initiate the contact. (That's changing, though, with more and more browser-based applications, especially social media, that scream for your attention when something changes.) You control those items that intrude on your attention by turning off or limiting the intrusion mechanisms. Control those that you initiate by limiting and consciously choosing the times to do so.

On and Off: The "information superhighway" has exits as well as on-ramps.

Key Takeaways

- A small investment in learning to search effectively will have a large payoff in both the result quality and the time it takes to find them.
- Learn to sniff out high-value links. If you're not sure a link will get you closer to the goal, revert to search.
- Don't keep checking scores, news, gossip, or what your friends are up to. Don't self-interrupt. Use tools such as aggregators and RSS to collect this information in one place where you can check it efficiently at the appropriate time.
- It's both blessing and curse that each "find," each valuable target page on the Internet leads to other interesting pages that will occupy way too much time... but only if you let it.
- Know when to say "Done." How much time will you allot for a given task? How deep do you really need to delve? How much detail do you need to deliver to others? Business decisions are made on partial, incomplete information all the time – starting with our inability to see the future.
- Create a memory chest for the nuggets you mine on the Internet and elsewhere. Software such as OneNote works very well as a memory chest.
- Ask for help occasionally. Offer help as well.

Coming Up...

The world of work is a complex ecosystem. How do you use off switches without upsetting the system?

Make the net that shall enmesh them all.
William Shakespeare, *Othello*

MAKING IT WORK:

THE DIY PRINCIPLE

Plans are useless...

...but planning is essential.

That's what Gen. Eisenhower said. He was right.

Let's plan how to implement some off switches.

COME ON,
I say,
and first **BEGIN**.

The time has come, to paraphrase Lewis Carroll, to talk of so much stuff: of elephants, cultures, and managers, of urgency, and good enough; of delegation, and of DIY, of diamonds in the rough.

DIY. Do It Yourself. Off switches won't come from your manager (unless she gave you this book). Rather, you take the lead, explore the off switches that fit your own situation, and start flipping them.

DIY plays out in two different ways in professional and knowledge worker environments. On one hand, there are so-called small businesses of a handful of people, or professional environments such as law firms that work in many ways like a cluster of small businesses. DIY is de rigueur here. You and the small team you work with own the culture, *are* the culture.

On the other hand, there are larger organizations with prescribed managerial hierarchies, cross-group collaboration that too often feels like competition, and an existing corporate culture like the water in which a fish swims, invisible, both supporting and constraining. To implement off switches as you navigate these cultural waters, you need a dose of DIY. Even the most supportive culture won't do it for you; you need to take the first steps.

We'll get to the elephants, cultures, managers, and the rest of the mock-Carroll inventory in the coming pages. They're all aimed at helping diamonds emerge from the rough by turning off a few switches and turning on a healthier work-work balance.

DIY. Do it. Yourself.

Start Now

Ask your kids, "How do you eat an elephant?"

They'll tell you, "One bite at a time"

There are a lot of suggestions in this book, many off switches and a few on switches.

Taken together, these off switches give you increased leverage over and control of your work life. Use them to increase your sanity level, reduce frustration, and provide not just work-life balance but work-work balance (p. 18). Trade the tense present for working and living in the present tense.

However, if you try to flip all of these switches at once, you'll add to your workload rather than subtract from it.

That's the eat-the-elephant problem.

You're can also find yourself overwhelmed by the size of the problem, paralyzed into inaction by the wealth of choices (p. 155).

Putting it off both compounds the problem and adds to your frustration, seeing the glimmer of a solution but unable to implement it.

On and Off: Choose neither "too much, too soon" nor "tomorrow and tomorrow and tomorrow...."

One Bite

Pick *one* of the off switches in this book as a starting point. Maybe it's turning off the buzzes and beeps of email (pp. 62 and 88, e.g.). Maybe it's improving the meetings you attend, or at least those you organize (pp. 108, 114, and more). Maybe it's finding at least a couple of 20-minute undisturbed task blocks each day (p. 104), or closing your real or virtual office door for a few task blocks (p. 130), or reforming the status reports no one reads (p. 128), or any of the other off switches of this book.

In fact, if you're skimming or browsing the book (it's perfectly fine to read it in ways other than cover to cover; it's not a novel!) and have landed here, look at just a few of the spreads referenced in the preceding paragraph. Find one that catches your fancy, that seems relevant to your working world, and... do it.

Start now.

The important thing is to make a start, to take a single bite. It doesn't matter which you start with. There are a few threads that weave through a number of off switches, in particular the 20-minute deep-focus task block and bane of partial attention. However, in general the various off switches are independent. You can improve meetings without fixing email, or work more effectively on the Internet without changing your smartphone habits. You can turn off more switches next week and next month.

But turn *one* off today.

> *Beginning in the middle, starting thence.*
> **William Shakespeare, *Troilus and Cressida***

Start With Yourself

This spread is aimed primarily at those who manage others.

Please don't treat off switches as a good idea to share with your team without experimenting with at least some of them yourself.

First, teams see quickly through managerial "do as I say but not as I do." (How do you feel when your own manager does this with you?)

Second, employees can best implement many off switches with managerial support –i.e., yours. If, for example, you call them five minutes after emailing to ask, "Have you read my email?" they'll find it difficult to turn off the email-all-the-time switch (p. 44 ff.).

Third, each work culture is different. As a manager and thus presumably a somewhat seasoned worker, you're better positioned to understand how the various off switches will play in your culture. For example, if meeting structure (p. 108) or always-carry-and-respond-to-your-Blackberry (p. 88) are prescribed by organizational fiat, your employees need your guidance on the right way to approach those off switches in your environment.

On and Off: Set a positive example for your teams, and share progress with your peers.

Flexibility in Corporate Cultures... and Managers

Neither the second barrier (managerial resistance) nor the third (organizational expectation) is written in stone.

If you're the manager, of course, you have the capacity to be flexible in your expectations. You can be open to "how" without compromising on "what," for example.

On p. 178 we'll look at influencing managers about off switches. If you're a people-manager, go read that now... and think about how to influence yourself first!

Even the most stringent organizational cultures leave room "around the edges" for incremental change.

If the mandate is a true top-down command, sometimes senior leaders can offer options that refocus the executive on accomplishments rather than the mechanics of accomplishing them.

In other situations, some avenues are blocked but others are open; for example, if email assumptions seem unyielding, work on shedding meeting waste or phone inefficiency.

By the way, my own experience is that even the most rigid email strictures may yield to at least some gentle and subtle changes.

You start.
William Shakespeare, *Henry IV pt. 1*

Your Direct Subordinates

Your subordinates, direct reports in particular, take their cues from you.

Learning From Their Manager (That's You)

Your team learns by watching you. Consider meetings. If you run meandering meetings, they'll receive an implicit message that such meetings are par for the course. They'll also have fewer opportunities to learn new ways by observation, which beats learning it from books (even this one!).

Let's say, however, that you recognize that your meeting skills aren't the best, at least for certain types of meetings (p. 112). Why not work together with your team to minimize meeting waste? Share your goals for better meetings, with or without noting that you're less than confident in your own meeting skills. Then offer them chances to run your team meetings, maybe rotating meeting leadership among team members.

Have a debrief session after a few meetings, perhaps over pizza. Ask them to employ these skills in their own meetings and share what they've learned with you and the team.

On and Off: The "secret sauce" to a great debrief meeting is *tomato* sauce... as part of a pizza.

Finally, try these skills out yourself at your team meetings and ask attendees for feedback; they'll appreciate your attempts at open improvement, and they'll almost certainly be supportive and encouraging.

Setting Managerial (Your) Expectations

Your team responds to your expectations, whether those expectations are reasonable in their eyes or not (see p. 139).

Consider email. If you're on your team's case about not responding instantly to your email requests, they'll be unable to use the biggest email off switch (p. 54). Likewise, if you send email at midnight or while you're on vacation, they'll be checking email at 12:30 a.m. or from the beach unless you tell them otherwise... and back that up with your actions.

By all means share this book's ideas with your team; having, say, eight people turn off the switches breaking work-work balance will add more business value than if you along throw those switches. However, they'll be limited in their ability to use the off switches unless you support them.

Set clear expectations. Get your team excited about the opportunity to get more done with less stress (or go home at a reasonable hour). Then support them, give them the monkey (p. 74), and get out of their way!

I myself at this time have employed him.
William Shakespeare, *Henry IV pt. 1*

Your Extended Team

If you manage a project or a group (your direct reports have people reporting to them), this section is for you.

With an extended team, whether that's a project team or a group, your influence over many team members is less direct. Instead of the two communication imperatives of the preceding spread, you have three.

Set an Example

Teams learn from managers: do's, not-do's, and transparency vs. hypocrisy (do as I say, not as I do).

Set Expectations

Communicate expectations clearly with your direct reports. For project managers, "direct reports" includes the leaders of each project sub-team, whether or not they report to you in the HR line-reporting sense.

Make sure you send the same message to those managed by people who report to you. Be conscious not only of the explicit message but the implicit meaning they'll draw from your actions.

On and Off: Set the example, and urge the true leaders on your team to do likewise.

Extend the Message

Who influences you more, your manager or your manager's manager? Your manager's manager probably sets the overall tone, but day to day you normally look more to your direct manager. (If you don't, what does that tell you about your manager? You can probably derive some "reverse lessons," valuable don't-do-it-that-way education.)

Encourage your leadership team, your direct reports or project leads, to take off switches to heart and extend them to their teams. If, for example, you have made it clear to your directs or leads that you foster work-work balance by not expecting them to be on email all the time (p. 58, e.g.), suggest that they pass the message on by both word and action.

Very Flat Teams (A Dozen or More Direct Reports)

Some organizations emphasize flat teams even among knowledge workers and professionals, where a manager has 12 or 20 or 40 or more direct reports.

Recognize that with this many direct reports, you must spread the message indirectly as much as you do directly. You need the most influential members on your team to connect with the others, just as if you were leading an extended team. (Even in less flat teams, some of your direct reports will have more influence than others, of course.)

They are reformed, civil, full of good, and fit for great employment.
William Shakespeare, *The Two Gentlemen of Verona*

Your Peers and Colleagues

Getting Buy-In From Co-Workers

In business, effective work requires coordination and cooperation with colleagues, peers, co-workers, and internal and external partners and customers.

To engage some of the off switches we've looked at in this book, you need help or at least buy-in from those people.

For example, let's say you've thrown the big email off switch, doing email in identified task blocks a few times a day (p. 54 ff.) rather than all-email-all-the-time. How do you let those you partner with understand that you're not being unresponsive to their emails, especially when they're used to seeing your near-instant replies?

In a peer meeting (e.g., your manager's team meeting) you might say, "I'm trying to take control of my Inbox so I can get more done. I'll normally be on email a few specific times each day. I could really use your help with this. If you need me more urgently, please feel free to call or even drop by."

Thus you enlist them not merely as observers but as partners and supporters of your work style.

On and Off: Not everyone has the same work styles... or will be inspired by the same off switches.

Promoting the Idea of Off Switches

How do you promote off switches to your peers, co-workers, and colleagues? Share, but don't proselytize.

I've had corporate co-workers try to sell me on all sorts of ideas over the years. Most of them had some merit, and I was always eager to learn, but... overzealous selling grated on me. I was glad they had found some toolset or method that was working for them; however, the overeager-puppy thing didn't match my style. I observed that it didn't go over that well with most others in the business or professional worlds, either.

Your mileage may vary, as they say. Still, the soft-sell tends to be most effective in these internal-influence situations.

As noted above, explain it simply. Enlist many or all of your peers and co-workers in your own quest. In most cases (absent serious office-politics infighting), they'll be eager to help you... and curious themselves about how it's going.

Give them updates occasionally. Engage their intellectual curiosity.

After a time, you may find them using some off switches too. And if someone should ask you where you came up with the idea, I'd be honored if you'd mention this book.

I have pleased my discontented peers.
William Shakespeare, *King John*

Working With Turn-Offs

What happens when your choice of off switches meets someone with whom you are uncomfortable? How does this work in an awkward business relationship?

If this difficult-to-work-with person is your manager, using off switches isn't your biggest problem. Solving these kinds of manager/employee issues is beyond the scope of this book. (See the next spread regarding off switches in more productive managerial relationships.)

First, consider whether you are dealing with a style difference (he loves all-email-all-the-time) or a personality disparity (you don't get along). Second, is the discomfort in discussing off switches and work styles mutual, or is it perhaps yours alone?

These situations call for different approaches.

Style Differences: If you have a style difference with someone, see if you can get him to acknowledge that his style is, say, always-on-email.

Don't suggest that his style is less effective than yours; people "comfortable in their skin" are often quite effective and productive.

On and Off: Don't force the issue. Establish your off switches in comfortable settings; expand from there.

Rather, can he accept that other people have different work styles? What are his concerns if you don't respond to his emails within 90 seconds? If he's worried about reaching you for urgent items, offer him your cell phone number and encourage him to use it. Discuss situations where you logically wouldn't be able to answer email anyway, such as meeting with a C-level executive or, for a lawyer, appearing in court.

In other words, try to figure out what his real concerns are, the reasons he wants you to respond in certain ways or avoid particular off switches. As with any negotiation, don't get caught up in positions; rather, focus on objectives or interests.

Hard-to-Approach Colleagues: Some hard-to-approach co-workers (or clients, etc.) truly are hard to approach, intentionally protecting their time and space. (That, too, is a type of off switch, though I believe there are better ways to accomplish such objectives.) Most of the time, however, it's your perception erecting the barrier.

One approach is to ask them for a bit of mentoring. Most successful people are happy to share a little of their expertise and experience. Discuss what you're trying to do, and ask them how you might best approach it. Often they'll jump right in and help! If it's a client or customer who insists on your never-switched-off appearance, help them see how your deep-focus work for them is really furthering their objectives. (Sometimes, you simply have to make exceptions for specific people, as noted on p. 66.)

I often had been miserable.
William Shakespeare, *Two Gentlemen of Verona*

Your Manager

Your manager may hold the key to your being able to throw many of the switches in this book.

Some off switches are pure solo plays, such as using a virtual door (p. 130) or reading email efficiently (p. 70). Others may require support from your manager, whether in the form of tacit acceptance or active engagement.

Managers provide air cover when, in street parlance, they have your back, particularly in response to an explicit request.

For example, if someone (at any level) complained to me that an employee in my department wasn't responsive to email, I'd ask for an example. Invariably the questioner would offer an item only a few business hours old. I'd explain our approach to email, and suggest that if their issue was truly urgent, they pick up the phone. (I'd ask for an example because it made for a clearer illustration, not because I didn't trust the folks on my team.)

I had various managers over the years after I figured out the email off switch. At an appropriate time, I'd explain my email approach in a no-big-deal way. Some were sympathetic, and I knew I didn't have to press; in other words, I had their tacit acceptance.

On and Off: Ask your manager about her own off switches if she has a sound work-work balance.

One said, "We should all do that," and recommended the email off switch to the entire team. That's an example of active (or even proactive) air cover.

Only one was skeptical. I asked him to try it out, saying I'd be glad to prioritize his and senior-executive emails (p. 66) if he thought it would be an issue. Eventually I won him over.

Take two steps before approaching your manager:

1. Select a particular small set of off switches, say one to three, with which you need her help.
2. Understand her style vis-à-vis these particular off switches. The more different her style, the greater the trust needed for her to actively support you, provide air cover, and so on.

If you have at least an informal mentoring relationship with your manager, you can enlist her help with the off switches you've chosen.

Be prepared to negotiate the parameters. For example, if she's all-email-all-the-time and you're working toward email task blocks (p. 56), you might agree to check email five times in an average workday rather than three, or to set alerts on email from specific senders (p. 66). If meetings with your manager are crisp (e.g., "be brief, be brilliant, be gone"), then state your goals briskly and request permission to try them. And if your culture is "better to beg forgiveness than ask permission," simply go for it!

What employment have we here?
William Shakespeare, *Twelfth Night*

Customers and Clients

You need to get on the same page with customers and clients in regard to your off switches

Almost every professional and knowledge worker has customers (clients).

By "your customers" I don't mean the people who purchase the products to which your team contributes, unless you're in direct contact with them. If you do work that is important to people outside your own chain of command, they are the customers of that work.

Customers can be demanding. And if your business depends on customers, you need to be sure unmet customer demands don't turn to customer dissatisfaction.

Raising customer satisfaction is difficult, but increasing customer *dis*satisfaction is rather easy. Ignore your customers, blow them off, pay them little heed, and your "DSat" levels will rise precipitously.

If you have a good relationship with your customers, communicating about your off switches will be straightforward. Remember that it's harder to "change the rules" on existing relationship than to establish ground rules at the outset of new ones.

On and Off: Some customers will push you just to understand your limits. Know and honor your limits.

One option is to let them know your goals with respect to email, desk phones and cell phones, meetings, and so on, and ask for their understanding and support. Offer to make an exception for them if they really wish; most will be generous and not take advantage of that offer.

Another option is to *gradually* dial back all-email-all-the-time habits. Recall the example on p. 44 about the perception vs. reality of responsiveness.

Along similar lines, don't show up at a customer meeting armed with a detailed, timed agenda (p. 110) if meetings to that point have been rambling, haphazard affairs. Ease into it. Suggest that together you try a slightly modified approach to what you've been doing; when that works, you can expand the effort a bit further.

Despite your best efforts, sometimes customers will demand your instant response on email, or insist on running a meeting inefficiently (or so over-efficiently that no actual give-and-take occurs). Be willing to make exceptions (see, e.g., p. 66).

Distinguish, however, between customers who don't trust (or respect the time of) anyone and those who don't trust *you*. You can do little about the former.

Start from latter viewpoint, though, and you'll be surprised how, once you've worked to truly win their trust, they move from demanding customer to supportive partner.

Are these your customers?
William Shakespeare, *The Comedy of Errors*

Home and Family...?

Are you checking your email over dinner? Does your smartphone buzz in your bedroom at 2 AM with mail from your boss? Do you and your still-at-home kids communicate more via Facebook than face-to-face? Umm... no, I won't go there.

Tying some off switches to home life is well beyond the scope of this book, and beyond my expertise as well. (Apply the meeting rules of p. 108 to domestic gatherings? Let's just say that wouldn't go over well with my family.)

What is in scope, however, is bringing work home. Don't allow work-work imbalance to cascade into work-life disproportion. Consider some options:

Email After Hours

These days, most professional and knowledge work lacks strict time boundaries, especially if your work connections span multiple time zones. It's often a necessity to do at least some email from home.

What's rarely necessary, however, is to do multiple email sessions from arrival time to bedtime. Instead, use the email off switch (p. 54). Treat email as a task for which you block time, once or perhaps twice a night.

On and Off: Develop clear expectations with family and colleagues about how much work you'll do at home.

For example, I often did two email blocks on weekday evenings.

I'd start with one task block after arriving and spending some time with my family; thus I would beat traffic by leaving the office around 4 PM when I didn't have late meetings, and yet I could still respond to end-of-day business needs.

A second brief session after my young kids went to bed allowed me to connect with Asia-based members of my team while they were in their offices.

The Omnipresent Smartphone

It's uncomfortable these days to leave your phone behind. However, it needn't interrupt you (p. 88).

Also, don't fall prey to the temptation of on-email-all-the-time because it's so conveniently clipped to your belt or waiting in your purse.

If you absolutely need to check in while on vacation, smartphones probably beat computers precisely because it's hard to work on them for long periods on them.

Working From Home

See the following spread for some suggestions on working from home during "office hours."

What, are you mad? I charge you: Get you home!
William Shakespeare, *Othello*

Working From Home

If you work from home at times (in lieu of going into the office), off switches are critical.

Don't allow home-based (or Starbucks-based) distractions to replace the interruptions of the workplace. The off switches of the workplace apply to the home office also, with some minor modifications.

Interruptions, Focus, and Task Blocks: If you're working from home, work from home. Instead of co-workers dropping by, though, now it's kids, spouses, neighbors, and even pets demanding attention. Within reason, don't allow them to steal your focus. (Obviously, working from home for a day or two to take care of a child who's ill, say, is a different story.) Set up task blocks just as you would in the office (p. 104).

While it's a good thing to take occasional breaks in any workspace, avoid home-related tasks that will interrupt you, from baking to buzzers on the clothes dryer.

Email: Set email task blocks (p. 58) just as you would in the office. It's tempting to check email regularly because you miss the interactivity of the office... and worry at least subliminally that they've forgotten about you. It's not worth it; use your time at home *more* productively than time in the office.

On and Off: Distinguish between obligatory (e.g., your kids) and self-imposed (e.g., email) interruptions.

That said, you may need to do email more frequently than you would in the office, at least at first. In some office cultures, managers worry about your focus and co-workers can be jealous (and snide). If that's the case, you need to be perceived as even more responsive when you're working from home, at least until you've established your *bona fides*.

However, such reactions are becoming less common as both managers and co-workers gain more experience with work-from-home.

Phones: If you have children at home, give co-workers and partners your cell phone number. Forward your desk phone to it. You should answer your "work" phone yourself rather than allowing a household member to answer it.

Conference Calls deserve your full attention, even when you're the only remote participant and you have trouble hearing the folks around the conference room table.

The Internet can pose at least as big a distraction at home as it is at work (p. 146).

The Office Itself: You need an office with a door (p. 130), real or virtual. Find a space that's comfortable, ideally one with a window and daylight, and designate it as a workspace.

Unless you're having Internet connectivity problems, the local coffee shop is a treat, not a substitute workspace.

She washes bucks here at home.
William Shakespeare, *Henry VI pt. 2*

Delegating: The Biggest Off Switch

Here, 184 pages into this book, we come to the biggest off switch of all, at least for those with managerial responsibility for people and/or projects.

It's also the hardest to implement.

Without question, delegation deserves its own book; this is not that book, of course. However, one of the many powerful arguments for learning to delegate effectively is the off-switch principle.

Your delegate's work returns time to *your* day. If your delegate is doing it, that's time you're not spending.

I'm not suggesting delegation is 100% freeing.

You will spend time assigning the task, checking the results, and perhaps overseeing some of the work coaching/training the delegate.

Nevertheless, you will spend less time on the task yourself – if not the first time you delegate an assignment to a particular person, then the times beyond that.

On and Off: Send an *empowered* delegate to meetings where your team needs a presence.

Delegation: Not Just for Direct Reports

Clearly you can delegate to direct reports, but you can delegate in other situations as well.

For example, project managers almost always delegate (i.e., assign tasks) to project workers who report to other managers. Not all project managers have that formal title, and not all projects are specifically called out as such. Nonetheless, if it's a connected series of tasks with a start, and end, and a goal, and if you're responsible for the result, then you're a project manager.

Your manager asks her direct reports to put together a budget for the coming year. You're the Excel expert, so she looks to you to collate the data. Presto, you're the project manager... but that doesn't mean you're the only member of the team. You can work out with your peers who does what, and when it's due. You're delegating horizontally.

You can even delegate up. I've seen a presentation specialist assembling a sales pitch delegate assignments to very senior managers, for example. The managers knew she understood the desired flow in ways that they didn't, and so they deferred to her expertise.

Tip: Be careful delegating over the heads of your direct reports to people who work for you indirectly. Think how it affects your plans when your own manager delegates work to one of your reports without at least consulting you first.

What is the news from this good deputy?
William Shakespeare, *Measure for Measure*

The Seductiveness of Short-Term Success

As you climb an organization's career ladder, you take on ever-larger responsibilities: longer-term projects, a shift from tactical toward more strategic work, accomplishing results through the efforts of others.

Slowly and subtly, you receive fewer positive strokes from immediate successes, for two reasons:

1. The results from the work often aren't visible when you complete *your* task on the work – i.e., outcomes lie in the future.
2. Often you are not directly part of any "completion event," where another worker, often a subordinate, performs the final task and sees "closure."

Rethinking the Peter Principle

According to Laurence Peter and Raymond Hull, people rise in an organization until they reach a position where they're no longer competent. However, perhaps focus is a bigger factor than pure competence.

That loss of focus comes in two forms.

On and Off: As a team or project manager, promote, recall, and revel in the successes of others.

First, a newly promoted manager is bombarded by new inputs, interruptions, and demands he doesn't yet know how to fulfill. Second, he goes home unsure what he's accomplished, since he's doing fewer short-term tasks with clear completion criteria.

In both cases he rapidly develops coping mechanisms. Often these mechanisms consist of finding tasks that he *can* complete directly and feel good about. He's seduced by short-term success… and doesn't know it.

Devised to handle the short-term overload of a new position, these coping mechanisms become ingrained strategies. After all, they're apparently working; they've alleviated the stress.

The Off Switch That Enables Strategic Thinking

There's a surprising simple off switch available to you if you're being seduced by the need for short-term success: recognize what's happening to you. Realize that you're trying to cope with new-responsibility overload. It's a normal situation, and a normal response.

At the end of the day, look back at the strategic irons you have in the fire. Consider tasks done some time ago that have only now come to fruition. They succeeded because of *you*, because of the work you did. When your team tells you what *they've* accomplished, those are your successes as well. Credit them for success, and you'll get credit as well.

This is old. What is the success?
William Shakespeare, *Antony and Cleopatra*

Urgent vs. Important

The seductiveness of short-term success, described on p. 188, correlates with an instinctive prioritizing of urgent matters... whether or not they are important.

Invest a few minutes in categorizing a day's worth of emails. If you can, copy all of a day's incoming emails to a separate folder. (In Outlook, use Advanced Options under Create a Rule: don't check a box on the first screen, click Next, then check "move *a copy*....")

A week later, consider the percentage of emails that were:

- Truly important and required your action
- Truly important but FYI, no action needed
- Business niceties ("thanks," FYI)
- Social, personal, etc.
- Not really important but requested action
- A total waste of electronic ink

Clearly you want to concentrate on the first two categories.

It doesn't take long to observe the business niceties once or twice a day, and a little goes a long way toward effective collaboration.

On and Off: Don't believe email's red "important" exclamation mark. Saying it doesn't make it so.

Personal and social ("want to have lunch?") mail takes up little time as long as you don't get mired in it; remember, email is a task (pp. 50and 54, e.g.), not an always-on stream.

It's the last two categories that drain time from the day.

It's easy, at least in retrospect, to spot obviously useless mails (spam, of course, but there's also a lot of neither-urgent-nor-important business-related mail). The real off switch lies in identifying urgent-but-unimportant and deflecting, deferring, or even ignoring it.

Email isn't the only way urgent-but-unimportant requests arrive, but it's a good place to start. It's also easier to handle such email than it is an in-person request.

The trick is recognizing that urgent and important are not synonymous. An issue can be urgent and important, of course, but the mere fact that it's urgent doesn't make it important.

Will it move the business forward? Does it correspond with one of your (or your team's) objectives? Indeed, is it truly urgent – that is, time-critical for the team or business – or is it just an item that's clamoring for your attention without true time pressure driving it?

Up next are ways to control urgent-but-not-important.

In time and passion, let's go by the important.
William Shakespeare, *Hamlet*

Play "D" to But-It's-*Urgent!*

Urgent to whom? Your boss? You? Or to the requestor?

Urgent is not the same as important, as noted in the preceding spread, though if your boss is the requestor that distinction can blur. But consider these questions before you take action:

- Is it truly move-the-business-forward important?
- Does it have to be done today?
- Does it have to be done by you?

Delete: Not Your Action Item

If you don't need to take action at all, delete it (or at least get it out of your inbox). Often you're copied on a request to someone on your team. Sometimes the sender is excited about some issue but hasn't requested specific action. Perhaps the request was sent to multiple recipients and it's not clearly your area of expertise.

(Sometimes there's business or interpersonal value in helping out on such a request. Jump in when *you* see value in acting, but don't feel put upon; it's your choice.)

On and Off: Turn off false urgency in your own requests as well as playing "D" on incoming items.

Delegate: Give Away the Monkey

If the request can best be handled by a member of your team, delegate it. Make sure you give the monkey away completely, however (p. 74). Don't sort-of-delegate where you still own part of the task. Make sure your delegate knows it's *her* item now. Let her know it's up to her to determine whether it's important and when (or even whether) to do it. In other words, as a manager make sure your team can recognize the difference between an assigned task and just passing something along. (And if you're not sure how to recognize the difference when it comes from your own manager, ask her!)

Defer: Ignore It, and It Will Go Away

You'd amazed at how many "urgent" items fade from view if they receive no response. There are times to put one of these items aside for a few days and see if there's a follow-up mail. Use your judgment, of course, based on both the content and the requestor.

Deflect: Give the Monkey Back

Someone else's fire may not be your emergency. One strategy for dealing with urgent-but-not-important is to give the monkey back. Seek clarification. Request more information. Ask, "When do you need this?" Often this strategy is a variant of deferring, especially when you believe the requestor is trying to dump something on you without any real business need behind it.

On, meddling monkey!
William Shakespeare, *A Midsummer Night's Dream*

Good Enough, and Good. Enough.

What's your standard? Excellence?

Great. But can you be excellent at everything you do, especially as you take on increased workloads and responsibility? And is every task worthy of excellence?

In the workplace, we clearly have major tasks where excellence should be the standard. However, we are also overwhelmed with tasks and mini-tasks that require not excellence but good enough. And in between those are tasks where the right standard is "Good. Enough."

Good Enough

Management expert Ken Blanchard once said, "Things not worth doing are not worth doing well." There are many business tasks that, if you really think about them, aren't worth doing, such as the urgent-vs.-important question of the preceding spreads. There are many more that are necessary but where increased quality won't improve business results.

On and Off: Excellence on business-critical items is more important than excellence on minor tasks.

The pursuit of perfection in items that don't justify it is similar to the fear you'll miss something if you use email off switches (p. 72). You may indeed miss something, just as you might approach perfection even on tasks where it's unwarranted. However, time isn't free. What could you gain from spending that regained time on other items, things of greater business importance (work-work balance) or even personal importance (work-life balance)?

The price of "excessive excellence" on unimportant items is the lack of time to be truly excellent when it matters. Even the most exacting jobs, such as aircraft design, have unexacting ancillary tasks. Also, as you move up in any organization, increasing responsibility necessitates not only that you pass many tasks to others but that you move rapidly through those where "good enough" is the appropriate standard.

Good. Enough.

Salespeople call it "selling past the close," pressing for a sale even after the customer has decided to buy. I called it the "Done" principle in *Legal Project Management*. When you're done with something, stop doing it. "Good enough" sometimes represents a minimum level of quality. Often you need more to truly complete a task. Then do it... and stop after you get there. "It's good, and it's enough" lies a few steps beyond "good enough." However, when "good" is indeed enough, switch it off and move on to your more important tasks.

He's a man good enough: He has one of the soundest judgments.
William Shakespeare, *Troilus and Cressida*

The Off Switches of Others

Throughout this book we've talked about *your* off switches. We've examined ways to convince others to honor and support them.

It's only fair that you support off switches that other people employ – not just those used by your team (p. 171), but the off switches of other co-workers, colleagues, customers, and clients.

The Benefit of the Doubt

For starters, give people the benefit of the doubt. Don't assume they're ignoring you, marginalizing you, or simply disliking you just because they're not responding instantaneously.

Consider that they may be using off switches, whether the ones I've described or others of their own invention.

Do you need an immediate response? Is it truly important, and not just urgent? Is the person you're asking really the right person, the one who has the information you need or the solution to your problem? If so, what's the right way to reach her? Does she prefer email for immediate items? Phone? A quick drop-by?

On and Off: Most people seek work-work and work-life balance... but may not seek it in similar places.

Likewise, if someone hasn't responded, or responded in an unexpected manner, try to understand his style. Some people don't respond directly. Perhaps he'll just do what's needed at the appropriate time. Maybe he's delegated it without copying you on the email (p. 193). Or maybe he's buried on business-critical matter of his own, or wrestling with a personal item, or simply out of the office unexpectedly.

Or perhaps his email crashed, or his voicemail failed; these things happen even in the most technologically astute environments

On the Margins

Sometimes people do get marginalized, written off by co-workers or even by whole organizations. Don't start by fearing the worst; give yourself as well as others the benefit of the doubt.

However, one common cause of marginalization in business environments is overwhelming people with urgent-but-not-important items. Discover and respect the off switches of your colleagues.

Off Switches vs. "Going Dark"

To "go dark" is to cease responding to business requests, often because you're not making the progress you expect of yourself. Going dark is not a proper off switch.

Live, and deal with others better.
William Shakespeare, *Cymbeline*

Mind the (Generation) Gaps

Generation Expectations

Once upon a time, only younger workers relied on email. Professionals had secretaries type their memos and even print out those new-fangled email letters. Then it seemed everyone in the organization used email, email, and more email. Go-getters traded their Filofax for a Blackberry.

Now new workers think Facebook and Twitter and texting are the way to go. They are surprised that *you* are surprised that they don't check email regularly.

These broad generalizations, of course, like any such blanket statements, are full of exceptions at the individual level. Still, they remind us that change alone is constant.

We are influenced most by our peers, scientists say (and any parent will confirm). Younger workers may use the email off switch not by conscious choice but because they don't view email with the same primacy.

On and Off: Few of us are born knowing how to focus. At any age, it's a learned and learnable skill.

There's no right or wrong, only styles and preferences. Find the off switches that work for you... and understand that those around you may choose differently not just from personal preference but because of generational influences.

Aging and Task Focus

Does the ability to deep-focus on tasks, with resiliency to interruptions, change with age?

I was intrigued that Mary Czerwinski, a principal at Microsoft Research, found that

...across many studies of interruptions and task switching, older individuals seem able to focus on their tasks more deeply, and are less likely to task switch when a notification comes in, than are younger participants. It might be informative to study the new generation of information workers coming into the workforce that have grown up with instant messaging, texting, and "always on" computing. [Might they] need to be trained to focus deeply on their work in order to make really good decisions?

We all have our strengths, whatever our age. We can build on our strengths, compensate for other areas, and, most of all, continually learn new ways to succeed.

Doing so will likely take all our attention. Turn off the interruptions. Let's get started.

Young Romeo will be older.
William Shakespeare, *Romeo and Juliet*

Summary

Off switches don't throw themselves. You need to find them, choose them, throw them. You need to support others in throwing off switches of their own, and you'll likely appreciate support yourself as you explore new options.

Remember that not all off switches work for all people, or at all times, or in all environments. What works with your manager might not work with a particular customer, for example.

The work environment is filled with subtle traps, gremlins who walk behind you resetting your off switches: urgent-but-not-important, misplaced perfectionism, even short-term successes.

On and Off: Don't forget the rule about eating the elephant. Don't try to do it all in one day, at one time.

Key Takeaways

- Eat the elephant one bite at a time: Start with a few off switches and go from there.
- Start with a few off switches, but start now.
- Support others in their use of off switches.
- It's often helpful to engage others in supporting your off switches, especially at the beginning.
- It's hard to break old habits; give it time. That said, if a particular off switch feels truly uncomfortable, it might not be right for you, or not right for you right now.
- Delegation is an off switch, a powerful one. Learn to delegate. Remember: those who can most help you learn to delegate are those who work for you.
- Don't get trapped in the rut of short-term successes if your job involves leadership or strategic issues. Switch off the need for short-term "strokes" when you succeed through others.
- Urgent is not synonymous with important. Play "D": Defer, Delegate, Delete, or Deflect.
- You're not too old, or too young, to start adopting off switches.
- Again, start with a few off switches, but start. Now. And do it... yourself.

Coming Up...

Here's where you take the reins and write the next chapter. Get out of the tense present. Move to the present tense, the "now" of deep focus and fewer distractions. Start using your off switches.

Come on, I say, and first begin!
William Shakespeare, *The Taming of the Shrew*

INDEX AND MORE:

LINE UP IN ALPHABETICAL ORDER

Index

Suggested Reading

Allen, David: Getting Things Done: The Art of Stress-Free Productivity. Viking Penguin, 2001.

> A highly specific and prescriptive methodology that works very well for some people. I don't use his method, but more than one colleague swears by it.

Berkun, Scott: *Making Things Happen: Mastering Project Management*. O'Reilly Media, 2008.

> His common-sense approach works for more than project management. His writing in general is always worth reading; start with *Mindfire*. A collection of articles he's written.

Blanchard Jr., Ken, Oncken, William, and Burrows, Hal: *The One Minute Manager Meets the Monkey*. William Morrow and Co., 1989.

> A highly readable condensed version of Oncken's theory of effective delegation. Even if you're not a fan of *One Minute Manager* storytelling, this book provides a full description of Oncken's "monkey management."

Carr, Nicholas: *The Shallows: What the Internet Is Doing to Our Brain*. Norton, 2011.

> A love-it-or-hate-it thought-provoking look at our relationship to technology in general and the Internet in particular.

Covey, Stephen R.: *The 7 Habits of Highly Effective People: Powerful Lessons in Personal Change.* Free Press, 1989.

A classic distillation of approaches to getting the right stuff done. Whether or not you're a fan of Covey's distinct style, this book can stimulate your thinking about leadership and time management.

Drucker, Peter F.: *The Effective Executive: The Definitive Guide to Getting the Right Things Done.* HarperBusiness, 2006.

If you're never read Drucker, this is a great place to start. But even if you've never read Drucker directly, if you've read any book on leadership or time/people management, you've read folks who were influenced by Drucker.

Freeman, John: *The Tyranny of EMail: The Four-Thousand-Year Journey to Your Inbox .* Scribner, 2011.

Interesting thinking on how technology is forcing us to adapt... not always for the better.

Horvitz, Eric, and Apacible, Johnson: *Learning and Reasoning About Interruption.* Microsoft Research, 2003. http://research.microsoft.com/en-us/um/people/horvitz/iw.pdf (or http://bit.ly/Lexician1072).

A technical study of recovery from interruptions.

Medina, John: *Brain Rules: 12 Principles for Surviving and Thriving at Work, Home, and School.* Pear, 2008.

The molecular science of interruptions. Really.

Oncken, William and Blanchard, Kenneth H.:
Managing Management Time: Who's Got the Monkey. Prentice Hall, 1987.

Lots of detail about Oncken's theories of delegation; you might want to start with the *One Minute Manager* distillation (above).

Oshry, Barry: *In the Middle.* Power and Systems, 1994.

Oshry is the leading thinker on power relationships in the corporate world. I'm on the fence about the Power Lab itself (I'm a graduate), but Oshry's analysis of organizational structure and culture change is outstanding.

Parkinson, C. Northcote: *Parkinson's Law. Houghton Mifflin, 1957.*

A classic, and an easy read. Look especially at Chapter 3, "High Finance," which despite the chapter title is really about the way we pay attention.

Peter, Laurence J. and Hull, Raymond: *The Peter Principle.* Souvenir Press, 1969.

The Peter Principle states that "in a hierarchy every employee tends to rise to his level of incompetence." Or hers. See p. 188 for my take on this idea.

Scott, Susan: *Fierce Leadership: A Bold Alternative to the Worst "Best" Practices of Business Today.* Broadway Business, 2009.

> Insights into effective discussions as opposed to just talking. ("Fierce" means committed rather than aggressive in Scott's formulation.)

Shakespeare, William: *Comedies, Histories, & Tragedies, Published According to the True Original Copies.* Jaggard and Blount, 1623.

> Okay, maybe no one actually reads the First Folio recreationally, but go catch up with Willy via your local theater companies. He's got a lot to say about leadership and time management.

Spool, Jared M., Perfetti, Christine, and Brittan, David: *Designing for the Scent of Information.* User Interface Engineering, 1997.

> Why the Internet works – and doesn't work – when you're looking for something on a site. Give it to your site designer. Once you understand why so many sites fail, you'll be able to find what you're looking for faster even on terrible websites.

About the Author

Steven B. Levy is a business leader, project manager, author, and the CEO of Lexician, which provides training, coaching, and consulting on people and project management and leadership.

Previously, he headed Microsoft's legal technology / operations department. He also headed two Microsoft product groups in his 17 years at the company. He specialized in innovation, leadership, customer and client focus, and team effectiveness.

His unique and practical approach to leadership, people and project management, and workplace effectiveness is based on 30+ years managing projects and leading businesses on three continents. His work has made him a highly requested speaker, trainer, and seminar leader.

His previous book was the groundbreaking *Legal Project Management: Control Costs, Meet Schedules, Manage Risks, and Maintain Sanity*.